THE PYRAMIDS SPEAK

By

Arthur Crockett

With additional material by
Wallis Budge, Olav Phillips, Stephen Ash, Bill Cox, Maria D'Andrea,
Timothy Beckley, Bruce Raphael and Sean Casteel

LET THERE BE LIGHT

i

THE PYRAMIDS SPEAK

By

Arthur Crockett

With additional material by
Wallis Budge, Olav Phillips, Stephen Ash, Bill Cox, Maria D'Andrea,
Timothy Green Beckley, Bruce Raphael and Sean Casteel

Published in the United States of America By
Timothy Green Beckley, dba Global Communications/Inner Light
Box 753 · New Brunswick, NJ 08903

Staff Members
Timothy G. Beckley, Publisher
Carol Ann Rodriguez, Assistant to the Publisher
Sean Casteel, General Associate Editor
Tim R. Swartz, Graphics and Editorial COnsultant
William Kern, Editorial and Art Consultant

Sign Up On The Web For Our Free Weekly Newsletter
and Mail Order Version of Conspiracy Journal
and Bizarre Bazaar
www.Conspiracy Journal.com

Order Hot Line: 1-732-602-3407
PayPal: MrUFO8@hotmail.com

CONTENTS

LET THERE BE LIGHT

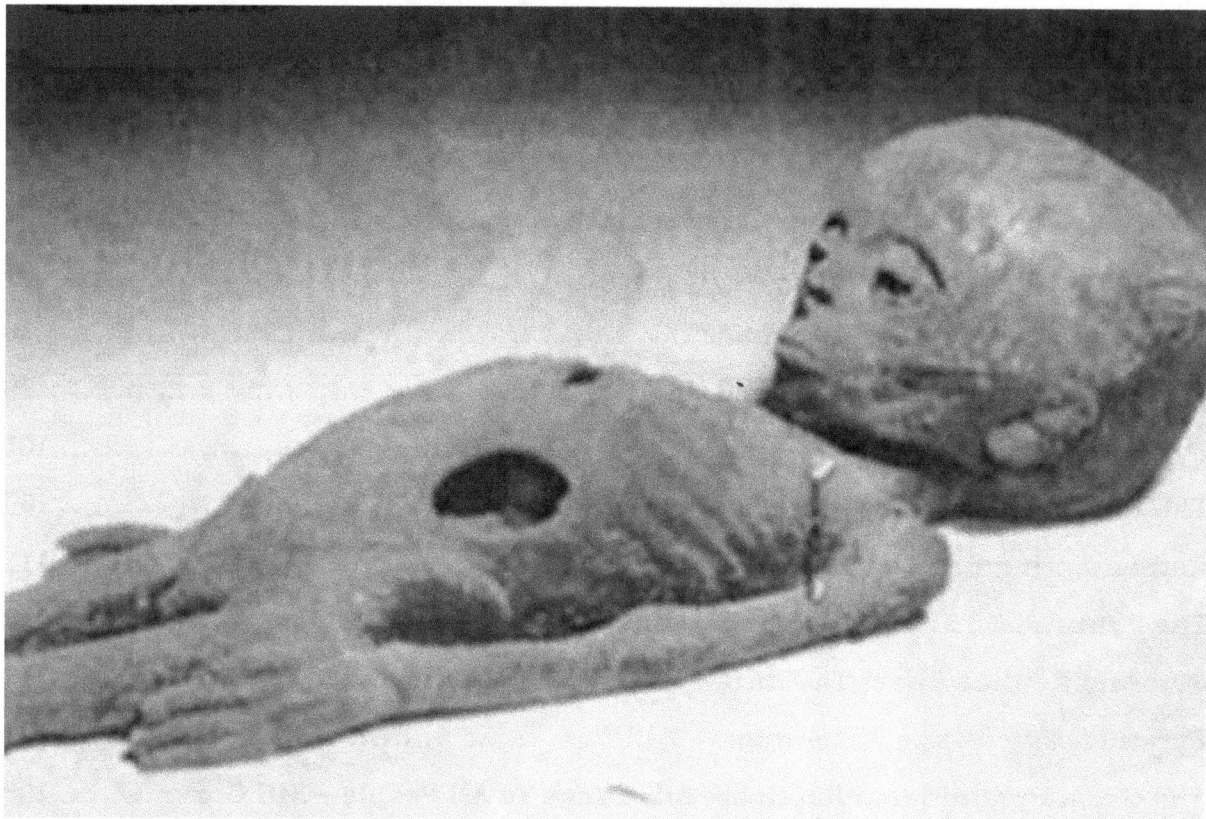

A strange story involving the Great Pyramid of Giza appeared in the March 2000 issue of the Egyptian magazine "Rose El-Yussuf."

According to the article, French Egyptologist Louis Caparat discovered this mummy in 1988 in a secret room of the Great Pyramid. The mummy "was found in a crystalline transparent case. At first, the alien appeared to be hibernating," or in state of suspended animation. It's believed to be a "humanoid," which is a hybrid of extraterrestrial and human DNA.

A papyrus found near the body tells of this being's encounter with the Pharaoh Khufu. Apparently, the alien convinced the Pharaoh to build the Great Pyramid as a tomb for this being after it had announced the future arrival of others of its species.

It was determined from the papyrus that the people who lived in Egypt during the Neolithic period were already very mixed, consisting mostly of people from the Mediterranean and blacks from Africa that were dolichocephalic (a Greek word meaning to have an elongated head).

As of this writing, the most recent news on the situation is that "Caparat sent a message to a colleague in Spain, Francisco de Braga, a biologist, inviting him to come to Egypt to take blood, cell, tissue and DNA samples from the dead alien." But when Dr. de Braga arrived in Cairo, he was detained by the Egyptian Ministry of State Security and put on a plane back to Madrid. According to "Rose El-Yussuf," the dead alien was taken to a laboratory at an undisclosed location by Egyptian military intelligence.

(Source: The Egyptian magazine "Rose El-Yussef," as relayed by "The World of the Unknown" in issue 283, April 2000).

iv

THE PYRAMIDS SPEAK

By Arthur Crockett

PREDICTIONS, WARNINGS AND SOLUTIONS

Within Egypt's borders, and in nearby Mesopotamia, civilization first flourished nearly 5,000 years ago. Oddly enough, Egypt contained many of the qualities that we hold dear in our own civilization. Egyptians believed, as we do, that the individual is a moral human being, that there is beauty and dignity in man, and that his soul survives after death. They believed that nature is something that is not only beautiful, but useful, and that it is extremely close to man. They had a well-organized system of government and were lovers of great art.

Yet, Egypt remains a land of mystery. There is prophecy in its great pyramids, magic in its fakirs, dire warnings in its adepts. The Egypt of today is being lost in the shuffle. Larger, more powerful nations nudge the country aside. But what they fail to understand is that Egypt, with its 5,000 years of wisdom, may have the answers to the insurmountable problems assailing the world powers. Let's examine the mysteries to see if the nation has something to offer the civilization of today.

DEMONS UNLEASHED

Not long ago an official in the Department of Antiquities in Cairo said that Egypt still had so many undiscovered treasures that if he could he would invite all the young archaeologists in every university in the world to come to the country and dig.

A wise statement? Not at all. In fact, if we can believe the strange and mystical Adepts of Egypt, the truth is that we should never have disturbed the tombs of the ancients.

THE PYRAMIDS SPEAK

AN ADEPT REVEALS A TERRIBLE TRUTH

Dr. Paul Brunton tells of meeting an Adept near the Tombs of the Kings. Brunton, who spent a lifetime studying mystics, yogis and holy men, reports on the experience in his book, *"A Search in Secret Egypt."*

We learn here that Brunton found the Adept sitting on a low boulder, cross-legged. Their eyes met and held for two full minutes. Brunton wrote: "Some hidden gland of latent clairvoyant vision inside my head, began to stir into sudden function., I saw a radiant spoked wheel of light revolve before me and slightly above my head, at high speed. With its working there was a receding of my physical moorings, and an entry into some supernormal and ethereal state of consciousness."

The Adept would not reveal his real name, saying that he could be called Ra-Mak-Hotep, yet he knew Dr. Brunton's name without ever having seen the man before. He called himself an Adept because: "It is a word which I prefer to any other; it was good enough for the ancients—including the Egyptians— and it is good enough for me. In those days the Adept was known and his status accepted; today he is practically unknown and the mere fact of his existence scornfully disputed. But the wheel will turn, and your century will be compelled to recognize that the law of spiritual evolution is ever at work, creating inevitably those who can freely function as spiritual beings no less than as material ones."

The Adept then told Dr. Brunton that he wanted to give the man a solemn message. He said: "Those who broke open the tombs of ancient Egypt have released forces upon the world that have endangered it. Both the tomb robbers of long ago and the archaeologists of our own days have all unwittingly opened the tombs of those who dealt in black magic.

"Every tomb which is unsealed lets out, like a flood, a rush of pent-up noxious evil spirit-entities upon our physical world. Each mummy that is taken out of such a tomb and transported to your European and American museums, carries with it the etheric link with those entities, and hence their awful influence. Those influences can bring only harm to the world, harm of various kinds, even to the point of destructively affecting the destinies of nations. You Westerners have no shield against them.

"Let it (the world) meddle not with the tombs whose psychic nature men do not understand. Let the world stop opening these graves until it has acquired sufficient knowledge to comprehend the serious results of what it is doing."

These words are not the complete message given to Dr. Brunton. The gist of it, however, was that opening the graves of the ancients did unleash terrible forces in the world.

THE PYRAMIDS SPEAK

The Adept mentioned the opening of King Tutankhamen's (King Tut) tomb, saying that this king possessed much occult knowledge and a spiritual soul. The opening of his tomb brought suffering on the violators; and also, in untraceable ways, on the world at large. In essence, this mysterious figure was saying that not all the ancients were peace loving, that many messed with things we know little about today.

TOMBS OF THE LIVING DEAD

The Adept went on to say that in Egypt some of the adepts who lived and moved in ancient times are still alive! Their bodies lie in a comatose state in certain Egyptian tombs which have not yet been discovered.

The Adept said: "The tombs of these great Adepts are too well-guarded and will never be found by your 'diggers.' Those tombs are not tombs of the dead, but of the living. They contain, not mummies, but the bodies of Adepts in a unique state which the word 'trance' most nearly describes. . . They remain fully conscious during their interment and although their bodies are in coma, their spirits are free and working."

The Adept explained to Dr. Brunton that the spirits of these buried Adepts move and travel and their minds think in a condition of full consciousness. The advantage they have is that they are aware of two worlds—the physical and the spiritual.

The Adepts have never had their hearts cut out, as is the case with mummies, and all of their organs are intact. Their stomachs have collapsed because of no intake of food, and their faces and bodies have been covered with wax, which was applied after they went into their trance.

The Adept told Dr. Brunton: "There is one Adept who has been in his tomb since 260 B.C., another since more than 3,000 B.C.; still another who has lain there for 10,000 years!

They are all working very actively in secret for the spiritual welfare of mankind. They know what is going on in the entire world, despite the fact that their bodies are interred. They are perfect men. By that I mean that their bodies cannot be touched—not even by any insect or parasite—such is the tremendous radiation of their spiritual forces. Moreover, they are in constant telepathic communication with certain living Adepts of our time who themselves possess a functioning body.

The spiritual treasures preserved by those ancient Egyptian Adepts are handed over to these living Adepts. When the time comes to awaken them, the ritual of arousal will have to be performed by one of the latter."

THE PYRAMIDS SPEAK

PROPHECIES OF THE GREAT PYRAMID

The Great Pyramid is also known as the pyramid of Cheops. It's located at Giza. The pharaoh Cheops was not the first builder of pyramids, but he was the greatest. He was also the most prophetic of all of the pharaohs, as you will see when we describe his pyramid. Scientists have noted that this great structure weighing six million tons has miraculously exact mathematical and astronomical measurements. What's more, the prophecies that lie within this giant have already been found accurate for the last four or five thousand years.

And incredibly, the prophecies yet unfulfilled have less than a century to run—and they are working out now in our own time!

PYRAMIDOLOGISTS REVEAL SECRETS OF THE AGES

Pyramidologists, those who study pyramids, are convinced that locked in these huge stone structures are occult secrets which must be aired for public knowledge. These students have spent their lifetime researching and writing many convincing tomes on the subject.

They are especially interested in the Great Pyramid, described by the Greeks as one of the Seven Wonders of the World. Unfortunately, these pyramidologists must work in the face of much criticism, and they cringe under the derisive title "pyramidiots." They have been doing so now for more than a century.

In fact, it was in 1859 that a London mathematician and publisher named John Taylor who discovered that the ancient Egyptians who actually built the Great Pyramid used the Polar Diameter inch to make their measurements. That is roughly the same inch measurement we use today in the United States and Great Britain. Taylor also said that "the Great Pyramid was built to carry a divine revelation or prophecy."

For more exacting proof we can go back to the tenth century, A.D., and find a writer (Arabian) who stated: "Surid . . . one of the Kings of Egypt before the flood, built the two great pyramids. The writer, Masoudi, refers the reader to Coptic history as his source. He said: "He (Surid) also ordered the priests to deposit within them (the pyramids) written accounts of their wisdom and acquirements in the different arts and sciences. . . with the writings of the priests containing all manner of wisdom, the names and properties of medical plants, and the sciences of arithmetic and geometry, that they might remain as records for the benefit of those who could afterwards comprehend them.

"In the Eastern Pyramid (the Great Pyramid) were inscribed the heavenly Spheres, and figures representing the stars and planets.

"The King also deposited the positions of the stars and their cycles; together

THE PYRAMIDS SPEAK

with the history and chronicle of time past, of that which is to come, and every future event which would take place in Egypt.

There are other Arabic manuscripts which tell of the same things about the Great Pyramid. They were written by Makrizi, Tohfat and Alagaib, and they speak of the pyramid as conveying knowledge of history, astronomy, and of records of prophecy.

One well-known present-day pyramidologist, D. Davidson, an engineer and tireless student, wrote a book titled, ***"The Great Pyramid: Its Divine Message."*** In it, Davidson says:

"In prehistoric times there existed a highly developed civilization, which suffered a catastrophic ending, a fact embodied in the traditions of various civilizations, in such legends as 'The Destruction of Mankind' of Egypt, 'The Destruction of the World,' of Mexico and Peru, and in Biblical lands and in China as 'The Deluge.'"

This civilization "on the edge of time," existed earlier than any other known cultures and researchers have established that its populace was highly advanced and the forerunner of later societies which thrived in various parts of the world.

THE GREAT PYRAMID'S DIMENSIONS

Pyramidologists put the height of Cheop's Pyramid at 484 feet and about 700 feet to a side, making the base circumference 36,524 inches. If you put a decimal point after the third digit of 36524 you get 365.24, the number of days in the solar year. Divide it by four and you have the base of each side, which 9131 inches, for the time between the equinoxes.

Divide that figure by 25 and you have the number of inches in the Egyptian and Hebrew cubit, and you again have 365.24, the number of days in the solar year. The sidereal year, twenty minutes longer, is also indicated. Likewise the "Anomalistic" year, which is about five minutes longer than the last. The Precession of the Equinoxes, a cycle which depends for its length upon the difference each year between the solar and anomalistic cycles, is expressed by these measurements for a period of 6,000 years, while modern astronomy knows them for only 400 years.

The pyramid also yields the exact value of Pi, a factor of great mathematical importance. The pyramid also reveals the sun's exact mean distance from the earth, the earth's polar diameter, and many other bits of astronomical data which can be found in expanded detail in readily available books on the subject.

One thing is certain: the designers of the Great Pyramid had a knowledge of astronomy which is equal to our modern times. Henry Mitchell, an American scientist and at one time a hydrographer of the United States Geodetic Survey, found that the Great Pyramid stands as nearly as possible to the exact central point of the globe.

THE GREAT PYRAMID IS NOT A TOMB

On the surface, it does not seem possible that the Great Pyramid was built for any purpose other than a tomb. Most of the great kings of Egypt had pyramids built to house their bodies after death. But such was not the case with the Pyramid of Cheops.

What we can surmise is that the designers of the Great Pyramid knew that the knowledge it possessed would likely die with them. Long centuries would pass before the scientists of the world learned what they already knew. There would be a materialistic culture, called the Roman Empire, and the Dark Ages. Finally, a civilization would appear which would examine the Great Pyramid and learn its secrets. This is the civilization we enjoy, which started some 500 years ago when Sir Francis Bacon was alive. Bacon threw out the formulas of Aristotle and turned to the study of nature, developing general laws from particular facts. It was the beginning of our scientific era—and surprisingly it is marked in the astronomical chronology of the Great Pyramid as coming between the years 1558 A.D. and 2045 A.D.

Engineer and author, D. Davidson, said: "The discoveries of Newton and Kepler and their successors all fall, therefore, within a similar category to that of the scientific revelation of the Great Pyramid. The latter, again, defines the chronological field of the former, which advances the pyramid science into a category of revelation infinitely beyond that defining the process of modern scientific discovery."

So, incredibly, the builders of the pyramid knew that between 1558 and 2045 there would be a civilization capable of reading and understanding their message! It is Davidson's stated belief that the Great Pyramid is not a tomb. Here he tells why he thinks so:

"The direct proof against the tombic theory is an engineering proof, and a definitely convincing engineering proof. The first Ascending Passage, which leads from the Entrance or Descending Passage into all the inner passages and chambers of the Pyramid, was and is closed by a tightly fitting granite plug or block at its lower or entering end. According to the exponents of the tombic theory, this plug was retained loose in the Grand Gallery, or elsewhere in the Pyramid's upper system, until the death of the king. The mummy case, it is alleged, was then dragged up the Ascending Passage and deposited in the King's Chamber; after which the granite plug was released and permitted to slide down from the Grand

THE PYRAMIDS SPEAK

Gallery into the First Ascending Passage to its lower end. Here, according to the theory, it came to rest, tightly wedged in, impossible to remove except by quarrying. In this position it effectively sealed access to the Upper Passages and Chambers. There the plug still remains sealing the access, and entrance to the First Ascending Passage behind the plug is gained only by means of Al Mamoun's quarried shaft which was excavated about 800 A.D."

It is interesting to note that the Arabian's workmen did not find any treasures or mummies. Davidson said there were ventilation shafts, two each for the king's and queen's chambers. Why would the dead need ventilation shafts? Davidson said, "As there was no need for these during construction, and as the chambers were sealed up when half the pyramid's masonry remained to be completed, it is obvious that the ventilation shafts were provided for the future, when the pyramid would be the subject of study by the people of a later civilization. The ventilation shafts in the queen's chamber were not completely cut through until 1872, by two Englishmen."

CHEOPS REAL GRAVE FOUND

In his book, *"The Lost Pharaohs,"* Leonard Cottrell wrote: "During 1924-1925 the expedition directed by Doctor G.A. Reisner, began to excavate the mastabas to the east of Cheop's pyramid (the Great Pyramid) where they found the cemetery of the royal family of Cheops, including three small pyramids built for his queens. Here, also, between the cemetery and the pyramid itself, were the foundations of Cheop's mortuary temple with its pavement of black basalt. Running through the cemetery was a large avenue which excavators named "Queens Street" because on its western side stood the three small pyramids of the queens. All of the tombs were ransacked by thieves.

THE GREAT PYRAMID'S STRANGE PROPHECIES

A builder's error was found in the construction of Cheop's pyramid. It's called the "displacement factor of 286." This error, which is the difference between the designer's plan and the actual base, is the reason that the top, or headstone, could not be placed.

In essence, the central axis of the entire passage and chamber system suffers a displacement of 286 inches from the central axis of the pyramid itself. But was it an accident? According to pyramidologists, the builders made no accidental error. They knew what they were doing, and they created that displacement with the hope that we would be clever enough to fathom the meaning. Some of us have!

Pyramidologists have figured out that if you count an inch as equal in time to one year, and then combine that with all of the mathematical and astronomical data collected, along with the "displacement factor of 286," you come up with some startling prophecies. For example:

1. The Great Pyramid in its Entrance Passage symbolizes the time from the construction to the time of the Exodus of Israel, which was from 2625 B.C., to 1486 B.C.

2. The First Ascending Passage extends from the point marking the Exodus, 1486 B.C., to the point corresponding to April 7, A.D., the date of the Crucifixion. From this point there are two passages. One—

3. The Horizontal Passage, leading to the Queen's Chamber, symbolizes the epoch of rebirth; the Jews rejecting the Messiah or Christ, and the Crucifixion date, the atoning sacrifice of the Christ. Then—

4. The Second Ascending Passage, or Grand Gallery, sometimes called the Hall of Truth in Light, continuing upward at an angle and symbolizing the Christian dispensation. This gallery, following the system of calculation used, dates the Great War (1914-1918). Actually, the prophecy runs from April 7, A.D. to August 4-5, 1914, when Great Britain entered the conflict, making it worldwide.

5. The Great Step at this point, a block of stone, is taken as symbolic of the consummation of the Age and the interpretation of the knowledge contained in the Pyramid. Here, we have arrived at the Great War period.

6. Next follows the First Low Passage, measured from August 4-5, 1914 to the 11th of November, 1918 A.D. This is a little more than four years and it coincides with the duration of the Great War-to the Armistice.

7. The Ante-Chamber, called the Chamber of the Triple Veil, measured from November 11, 1918 to May 29, 1928. Here the stooping posture of the Low Passage can be changed to an erect position. This interval is described as "Truce in Chaos," a ten-year respite from the terrible horror of the Great War, brought about by divine intervention, which shortened what might have been a continued period of unbearable tribulation from 1914 to 1936, twenty-two years instead of four. Otherwise we would have had a situation described in the Bible as "no flesh would have been saved."

8. The Second Low Passage, extending from the 29th of May, 1928, to the 15-16th of September, 1936, is symbolic of the Final Tribulation and evidently coincides with the Great Depression and the smaller wars of the period.

9. The Second Low Passage leads to the King's Chamber and symbolizes the period from 1936 to 1945, a grave period on earth marked by World War II. The King's Chamber is also known as "The Chamber of the Grand Orient," which figures prominently in the Second World War since the Japanese and the Chinese fought bitterly long before the war worldwide started. The year 1936 was crucial in the Chinese-Japanese conflict.

THE PYRAMIDS SPEAK

10. In the chamber known as the "Passion of the Messiah," the symbol expresses itself as a period from 1945 to 1985, in which the atomic age is ushered in and in which a series of crippling recessions assail the world.

11. In both of Cheop's cartouches, located at the base of the pyramid, pyramidologists have calculated that the ancient Egyptians who planned the great monument foresaw great tribulation from the period of 1985 to 1999. Foretold are wars and famine, pestilence and disease. They see a dire threat to civilization as we know it, yet one that is saved from extinction by the appearance of a Messiah.

12. The period of 1999 to 2045 is covered in the "Hall of Judgment," the Cleansing of the Nations, the Return of the True Light from the West, the literal Presence of the Master of Death and the Grave. At this point it is proclaimed that Death is swallowed up in Light. The interpretation is that this period, 1999 to 2045, will be a period of hope and of rebuilding.

There are no measurements or prophecies beyond 2045. Does that mean that the end of the world will come at that time? We can't say for sure, but it could mean that the great prophets who designed the calculations knew that things on earth would be so different after this point that they knew it was useless to speculate beyond a certain date. Could this represent "Judgment Day," or some other turning point in history? We think so!

INCREDIBLE PROPHECIES IN EGYPTIAN TAROT CARDS

You've seen a Tarot deck and you may have even had your fortune read by a gypsy using Tarot cards. We can't vouch for the accuracy of a fortune-teller's predictions, but what we can say is that these cards, which were invented by the ancient Egyptians, have accurately foretold the history of the world from about 100 years before Christ to the year 2100 A.D.

The most fantastic aspect of this phase of Egyptian lore is that the book containing the Egyptian game of Tarots miraculously escaped the devastating fire at the Alexandrian Library when Julius Caesar invaded the country. If it had been reduced to ashes, we would have never been aware of the amazing prophecies the cards hold.

There is no question about the origin of the cards. On "The Wheel of Fortune," the tenth card, there is a sphinx. If you look at the second card, "La Papessa," you will see that the name points to a connection with the East, where the High Priestess was in antiquity a part of the state cult. It is interesting to note here that despite the fact that the Tarot cards made their debut in Italy, Spain and France—all Catholic countries—the title of the second card, "La Papessa," was considered blasphemous.

THE PYRAMIDS SPEAK

Originally, there were 78 playing cards made up of 22 Tarocchi and 56 cards marked with figures and pips in the four suits. With the passage of centuries, however, the 22 Tarots and four Knight cards were dropped from the deck, leaving the 52 cards we are familiar with in a regular deck.

Ancient Egyptians used the 78 cards strictly for fun and gambling. The designers whose origins we can only speculate on, had already made their prophecies in the designs, so there was nothing more for them to do. The cards first appeared outside Egypt at about 1325, and the gypsies had nothing to do with bringing the Tarots out of Asia. In fact, the cards had already been in circulation for about 100 years when they appeared in Paris in 1427.

In Italy, in the 14th Century, the cards were called Naibi; in Spain, Naypes. Oddly enough, these non-Latin names came from the Arabic Nabi—and that means prophet!

RIDDLE OF THE TAROT CARDS

As we said earlier, the second card, "La Papessa," was an affront to the Christian Church. The name of the cards in Arabic, Nabi, was a profane word to the Islams, who did not take kindly to anyone or anything using the word "prophet" lightly. Further, the Arabs did not use the cards because the Koran forbade gambling.

The feeling among researchers is that these symbolic tablets had their origin about the time the pyramids were first put up, and that from there they were received by high priests in the Order of the Temple, who may have gotten them from highly advanced beings who had landed here from another planet or a representative of some secret order with ties to ancient Atlantis It is known that the path of the Tarots went from the pyramids to Baalbek, on to Acre, and then to Paris, the seat of the Order of the Temple. In fact, the word TARO may be an anagram for the Order of the Temple, ORTA.

HOW THE TAROTS BEGAN

During the reign of Napoleon III, the Librarian of the Ministry of Education, Christian Pitois, wrote in his book, "Historie de la Magie," that the Egyptians were forced to devise a method of retaining knowledge because they considered themselves doomed.

Pitois wrote: "The initiate sees a long gallery supported by caryatides in the form of twenty-four sphinxes, twelve on each side; On each part of the wall between two sphinxes there are fresco paintings, representing figures and mysterious symbols. These twenty-two pictures face one another in pairs.

A time followed when Egypt no longer able to struggle against her invaders, prepared to die honorably. Then the Egyptian savants (at least so my mysterious informant asserts) held a great-assembly to arrange how knowledge, which until that date had been confined to men judged worthy to receive it, should be saved from destruction."

According to the Librarian, the most important scientific secrets were engraved on small plates, the Tarot. It's likely that until the 14th Century the cards were held by the secret orders of Egypt, Syria and Palestine. And, of course, the Order of the Temple.

But tragic times fell on the Templars. In 1291 their citadel at Acre was captured by the Sultan of Syria. Then on October 13, 1307, "Black Friday," the entire Order was crushed by the King of France and the Pope of Rome. It was a brutal massacre of the Knights Templar, but a few survivors were wise enough to know that if the cards were to continue in the world, they would have to be given to gamblers. Their theory was that vice would preserve the ancient Egyptian cryptograms for generations to come. They were right.

HOW THE TAROT TIES IN WITH ASTROLOGY

Researchers feel that the Tarot plates were made some time before the Roman occupation of Egypt in 47 B.C. They don't know the exact date. What they do know is that the zodiacal cycle of Pisces was opened in the year 100 B.C. In the precession of the equinoxes the sun retrogrades through the twelve signs of the zodiac at the rate of about 2,000 years in each sign. The wise priests of Egypt felt that the year 100 B.C. was the logical time for them to leave a message for future ages.

You can see a historical connection between Egypt and the Tarot cards when you examine the last card, Il Mondo. Also known as the Universe, the card displays the cardinal signs of the zodiac—Aquarius, Scorpio, Leo and Taurus in the four corners of the card in the form of an angel, eagle, lion and bull. The sphinx is shown on ancient frescoes with a human face, body of a bull, legs of a lion, and wings of an eagle.

This is the "cosmic" card, proclaiming the astronomical and astrological significance of the Tarot cards. Whether you believe that the stars influence our lives or not, you do have to agree that the sun, moon, planets and stars are sources of radiation which exercise influence on the earth.

A. Gangnus wrote in the Russian magazine, *Znanie-Sila*, "In ancient times astrologers attempted to predict the future by the respective positions of the planets. Who knows, this may not be so absurd. If the respective positions of the planets really influence the sun, then astronomical tables could become data for heliogeophysical and even long-range climatic forecasts."

THE PYRAMIDS SPEAK

American scientist William F. Corliss says, "Stranger still is the observation that sunspot maxima are roughly synchronized with the French and Russian revolutions, both world wars, and the Korean conflict. If there is some small truth in astrology, the thing to do is to explain this truth in scientific terms and strip away all pretense." It has already been established scientifically that the number of car accidents increases four times on the second day after solar flare-ups. Also, during the periods of violent explosions on the sun there is a sharp increase in suicides, jumping four to five times higher than the normal rate.

THE MYSTERY OF THE TAROTS

There are 22 Tarot cards representing the 22 centuries of the Piscean age. The Tarot is actually a history in the form of a calendar, with each card representing the event of a century. The symbols are amazingly accurate with the century each displays. The examples used here are from the Italians deck of the 14th Century, which is the oldest specimen, historically.

IL BAGATTEL

This is the Magician's card. He stands in front of a table which holds four symbolic articles—a cup, a coin, a rod and a sword. You can see Osiris with "djed"—the tree trunk. The four objects on the table are the four "Children of Horus," the cardinal points which accompany the images of Osiris. Osiris was savagely slain by Typhon, but he rose from the dead. In the Book of the Dead he says: "I am the resurrection. In hymns written to Osiris you can find the words, "I have not done evil to mankind. I am pure."

This card clearly depicts the first century before our era. It is the time of the Magi, the Ancient Mysteries, the Teacher of Righteousness of the Dead Sea Scrolls. The first Christians, affiliates with Essenes, used the sign of the fish, symbolic of the Piscean Age.

LA PAPESSA

The High Priestess card. This stately woman is pictured sitting on a throne. She wears a tiara and a mantle. There is a cross on her chest and a book on her knees. This is the card that covers the first century of our era, from the birth of Christ to 100 A.D. It depicts the Church with its tiara, cross and Bible, and represents the formation of the Christian Church.

L' IMPERATRICE

The third card is called the Empress. She sits on a throne. She is crowned, holds a scepter and a shield emblazoned with a hawk. The symbolism here is the grandeur of Rome when it flourished supreme. It typifies Hadrian, the Emperor builder (76-138 A.D.) and Marcus Aurelius (121-180 A.D.), the philosopher-king.

THE PYRAMIDS SPEAK

L' IMPERATORE

The Emperor card. He sits on a throne holding a scepter. At his side is a shield with an eagle. His legs are crossed. At the dawn of the third century, which this card represents, a decision was made by the army to elect a Roman Emperor. The man was Diocletian (245-316 A.D.). He made great attempts to stabilize the Empire. It is felt that the crossed legs allude to Christianity because it was in this century that a reign of terror broke out over the first Christians.

IL PAPA

This fifth card is called the Pope. It shows the Pope's right hand making the sign of the cross. His left rests on a triple cross. Two holy men face the Pope. The ancient Egyptians accurately forecast here the establishment of Christianity as the state religion by the Council of Nicea in 325 A.D. By 300 A.D. Christianity had already become the official religion of Britain.

GLI AMANTI

The card is called the Lovers, and also TWO WAYS. It shows a young man standing between two young women at a crossing. One of the women wears a diadem and a mantle. The other is shown with a wreath of flowers and a light dress. This was a perfect depiction of the separation of the Eastern and Western Roman Empires, which occurred in the fifth century. The woman wearing the long robe is the West, or Rome. The other, with the garland in an exotic dress, is the East, or Byzantium.

IL CARRO

This seventh card which covers events in the sixth century is the Chariot card. It shows a two horses. He holds the rod of in the other. Two crescents are the charioteer. This warrior is warrior in a chariot drawn by power in one hand and a sword attached to the shoulders of Mohammed, born in 570 A.D., wearing crescents, which are the badges of Islam. The age also produced Emperor Justinian who codified Roman Law.

LA GIUSTIZIA

The Justice card. A woman wearing an iron crown carries a sword and scales. She is the law of Islam, carried by the sword in the name of Justice. This woman depicts our own symbol of Justice. Here, in the seventh century, the card depicts the rise of the Arab Empire.

L' ERMITA

The ninth card is the Hermit. An old man is seen with a lamp and a staff walking in the night. It is the symbolic picture of Islam obscured by the battle of Poitier-

THE PYRAMIDS SPEAK

Tours in 732 A.D. The old man depicts the decline of the Arab Empire.

RUOTA DELLA FORTUNA

The tenth Tarot card is the Wheel of Fortune." You see a monkey and a dog turning a wheel. A sphinx with a dart hovers above. The Wheel of Fortune turns with the crowning of Charlemagne in 800 A.D. In this century the rule of the Divine Right of Kings is established to last for a thousand I years. Feudalism becomes a permanent institution. The beginning of learning in the Occident (West)— the Carolingian Renaissance—is portrayed by the sphinx, which is the eternal symbol of wisdom.

LA FORZA

In English it is the Force card. The picture shows a woman with a long mantle and a wide-brimmed hat. She is taming a snarling lion. The eleventh card for the tenth century concerned itself with the Church. The woman's garb tells us that it is the Church's ecclesiastical costume. The lion represents royalty, so we can see at a glance that in this century there will be two factions, the Church and the State, at odds with each other. If you examine the history, you will see that the prophecy was correct. Pope John XII crowned Otto of Germany in 962. One year later the Pope was deposed by the Emperor. The conflict between the Church and the State climaxed in the next century when Henry IV was shamed at Canossa by Pope Gregory.

L' APESSO

Here you see a hanged man. A night sky is the backdrop, with a half-moon and a gallows. The man's hands are bound, but he is not hanging in the conventional manner; he hangs by one leg. The other leg is bent so that the two form a cross. The crossed legs symbolize the trials of Christianity in this century, and there were many. It started off badly for the Christian in 1009, with the profanation of the Holy Sepulchre by the Mohammedans. At the end of the century, 1099, the Crusaders occupied Jerusalem. The crescent moon alludes to Islam—and during this period Christians and Mohammedans were slaughtered by sword or died horribly through sickness.

LA MORTE

This is the Death card. Number 13 holds a prophecy for the 12th century that is amazingly accurate. A skeleton armed with a scythe is shown using the tool to lop off heads. This card can apply to the crusades that were fought and to the fact that Saladin gained control over Jerusalem in 1192 after a bloody battle. The skeleton with the scythe, however, more closely depicts Genghis Khan (1162-1227), whose armies swept out of Mongolia and left a bloodbath all the way to the Adriatic.

THE PYRAMIDS SPEAK

LA TEMPERANZA

An angel with two urns pours a liquid from one vessel into the other. It is the century of Temperance. Governments finally introduce temperance into their systems to make for a better world. The thirteenth century, symbolized by pouring old wine of classical culture into the empty urn of medieval darkness. It was during these years that the Renaissance was born. Dante (1265-1321) introduced to Europe the classic ideal of happiness in his book "New Life." Roger Bacon saw the fallacies in the old scholars' works and opened the age of science. The Magna Carta (1215) came into being. Marco Polo sailed to Asia and bridged the gap between the East and West. Because of Polo, Europe was introduced to many new ideas. The allegory is therefore quite plain when you look at the angel pouring a substance from one urn to the other.

IL DIAVOLO

The Satan card. You see a horned monster with bat wings. He holds a burning torch and stands on a pedestal. Two satyrs are chained to it. The ancient Egyptians were on the mark here. The two satyrs represent England and France. The devil used his torch to touch off the Hundred Years War that was waged between those two countries. But that wasn't all the Egyptians saw for the 14th century. The bat wings were black, and spread wide to cover all of Europe during the Black Plague of 1347 to 1350.

LA TORRE

The sixteenth Tarot card stands for the Tower. There is a tower here being struck by lightning. You see a man wearing a crown falling from the top. A monk has already fallen and is lying on the ground. It's not difficult to guess what the Egyptians saw for this century. Gutenberg discovered printing, and because of it the light of knowledge was spread everywhere. However, the Church and royalty suffered. Europeans learned how to read, and thus speculate. Free thinking was fatal to dogma. The old concepts were shaken, just as the lightning shook the tower. Christopher Columbus discovered America in 1492, opening a new world of promise as opposed to the Old World of decay.

LE STELLE

The card is the Star. Brilliant stars shine in the sky. A nude young woman sits on a river bank. She has two vessels. Water pours down. Nearby on a bush is a singing bird. The stars on the card are appropriate. This is the century of the astronomers. Copernicus died in 1543. Tycho de Brahe was born in 1546, and Giordano Bruno in 1548. Kepler was born in 1571 and Galileo in 1564. The allegory of the two vessels are a metaphor for new times—the Reformation. Martin Luther, who died in 1546, attempted to purify Christianity. This was the Elizabethan era. Intel-

15

lectual horizons expanded beyond the globe. Francis Bacon made amazing strides in modern science.

LA LUNA

The 18th Tarot card is full of symbols. Egyptians certainly must have seen this 17th century unfolding before them because they pinpointed everything that happened in that century. This is the Moon card. You see it partially obscured by dark clouds. The twilight is pale. A dog and a wolf bay at the moon. A pool in the foreground is marked by a crawfish emerging from the water. It is a truly sinister card, and it accurately depicts the Thirty Years War (1618-1648) between the Catholics and the Protestants. The picture also shows tears or drops of blood falling from the moon's face. In those days, crawfish ate the dead bodies on the battlefields. In 1665 England suffered the plague. One year later the great fire destroyed four-fifths of London. England also saw a Civil War in this century, plus the rule of Cromwell (1599-1658). Blood and tears on the moon were really prophetic.

IL SOLE

This is the Sun card. Shown here are a boy and girl playing in a garden in front of an unfinished wall. The sun above sheds tears. Ironically, this was the century of Louis XIV, the Sun-King. The unfinished wall may depict the construction of Versailles, France, a splendid edifice yet built at the terrible cost of the suffering of the common people. The boy and girl could mean Louis XVI and Marie Antoinette playing in the park of Versailles, unaware that they will be central characters in the French Revolution. Also prominent in this era were Peter the Great, Frederick the Great, and Catherine the Great. There was good reason for a grieving sun.

IL GIUDIZIO

The Judgment card shows an angel with a trumpet soaring in the clouds while three figures—a man, a woman and a child—rise from an open grave. The period has often been called the Era of Revolution. Ancient Egyptian prophets writing in their Script of Destiny saw this 19th century actually beginning in the latter part of the 18th. It includes the burning of the Bastille in 1789, and the American Revolution from 1775 to 1789, when George Washington took office as the first President of the United States. The three figures rising symbolizes the rise of the Third Estate, which is the common people. Revolutions in the 19th Century were almost common. France had three—1830, 1848, and 1871. Insurrections occurred in Prussia and Austria in 1848; Italy had two, 1848 and 1860. Then there was the Paris Commune in 1871. The lower classes rose up, just as depicted in this card, in the end of serfdom in Russia and the abolition of slavery in the United States.

THE PYRAMIDS SPEAK

IL MATTO

This is the Fool card. The picture certainly describes the 20th Century. It shows a gaily-dressed man in a fool's cap carelessly stepping into an abyss. A dog, sensing the danger, tries to grab him by the leg. The jester carries a stick and a bag.

The Egyptians were well-aware of our foolishness in the 20th century. We've had two world wars which devastated entire nations. We've had a Korean War and a Vietnam War, both of which were bloody and suicidal. This century has seen more than 200 smaller conflicts since the United Nations was formed.

Great Britain was just engaged in a conflict with Argentina. The United States in Lebanon and Grenada. Russia in Afghanistan Iran and Iraq are fighting. So too is the I.R.A. with the British in Ireland. Israel fought bitterly against the PLO. At no time in history have wars been so numerous, costly, and stupid.

And the intriguing question now is: What does the jester carry in the bag as he steps off the precipice? Could it be a nuclear explosive device? It has already been stated by high officials in many countries that if a nuclear war does come it will be because someone somewhere presses the wrong button. And who might that be? A fool, of course.

We should fear the fool; Jesus certainly did. It was said: "Once Jesus was seen walking down a road in great haste. People, astonished at so unusual a behavior, followed Him, asking:

'Why art Thou hurrying? Whom seekest Thou?' Jesus took no notice of them and continued on His way, hurrying. So they persistently cried: 'But in these places there are no wild beasts, no lions, no panthers, wolves! What is it that is chasing Thee?' Then Jesus answered: 'I am running away from the fool!' 'But art not Thou the Christ? By the power of the Holy Ghost Thou canst blow on that man and he will become wise.' Jesus replied: 'By the breath of the Holy Spirit I can blow on the ignoramus and he will become all-knowing. I can breathe upon a blind man, and he will regain his sight. I breathe upon a dead man, and he comes back to life. But I breathe a thousand times upon the fool, and he still remains a fool—this is why I am running away from him.'"

IL MONDO

The last card is a cryptogram for the 21st Century and is called The Universe. Egyptians promised a Golden Age here after the arrival of a new race of beings from cosmic space. The card shows a virgin in a garland holding a wand and walking on clouds. The four corners of the card hold the four signs of the zodiac— Aquarius, Scorpio, Leo and Taurus. There is a cosmic tone to the card, making it logically The Universe. The woman is Isis, the Egyptian Madonna. In Egyptian folklore, Isis found the severed parts of her husband, Osiris, along the Nile. She put the parts together and wrapped them mummy-fashion and brought him to life. Symbolically, this is the unification of the world. Mankind therefore in the next century will reap the joys of Brotherhood and Unity.

Virgil also saw the coming of a new race from the heavens, because he wrote in his Cumean Prophecy: "The last era of Cumean song is now arrived and the grand series of ages begins afresh. Now the Virgin Astraea returns, and the reign of Saturn recommences. Now a new race descends from the celestial realms. Do thou, chaste Lucina, smile propitious to the infant boy who will bring to a close the present Age of Iron and introduce throughout the whole world the Age of Gold. Then shall the herds no longer dread the huge lion, the serpent also shall perish and the poison's deceptive plant shall die. Come then, dear child of the gods, great descendant of Jupiter! The time is near. See, the world is shaken with the globe saluting thee: the earth, the regions of the sea, and the heavens sublime."

CULT OF THE DEAD

Life after death and ceremonial magic has always meant a great deal to the Egyptians. During the New Kingdom, also known as the Empire, which lasted to 1089 B.C., there was almost an obsession with death. Life on earth was of little importance to the Egyptians. Their hopes were pinned on what lay after.

Egyptians were totally preoccupied with preparations for death and were obsessed with ceremonies, rites and magic. Priests were considered the spokesmen for the gods; those people who did not receive the blessings of priests could not expect to succeed in their endeavors. Priests were the wise men. They had a knowledge of writing, astronomy and the occult. They also knew all there was to know about ceremonial magic, which brought supernatural forces into beneficent action; and black magic, which was used against transgressors. The 19th century British Egyptologist Sir Wallis Budge said that "magic was made to be the hand-maiden of religion." That has no basis in truth now, but in the New Kingdom it hit the nail squarely on the head.

This obsession with death lasted only a few centuries. Eventually, Egyptians grew away from thoughts of death and concerned themselves with living. Yet, during the New Kingdom it can safely be said that the religion of the age was truly a cult of the dead.

MAGIC TALISMANS AND AMULETS

Protection from demons was, and still is, important. Magic amulets were designed to keep the wearer from the dangers of natural forces and supernatural evils. Many of them were buried with the mummy and were called guardian amulets, often an amulet for every organ and limb. Others were placed in the tomb to ward off putrefaction, worms, tomb robbers and mildew. The heart of the dead body was removed and preserved separately, and in its place a carved stone amulet, sometimes heart-shaped was fitted. This was done to prevent the real heart from being stolen by a demon.

THE MYSTICAL SCARAB

Early in Egyptian history the scarab amulet became the most popular of all talismans. It was modeled after the dung beetle. More importantly this scarab became the symbol of the god Khepera, who was the creative force behind keeping the sun on its daily path. The scarab received even greater distinction when the pharaoh Akhnaton established the monotheistic religion of sun worship. The scarab then became the symbol of the Supreme God.

The scarab amulet meant life. Its presence on or in a dead body represented the potential life in the body. The magic spell carved on the amulet usually requested immortality for the wearer. Eventually, everyone wore one, dead or alive. In fact, the dung beetle itself was thought to achieve fertility for barren women who dried and powdered the insect, then drank it in a mixture with water.

STRANGE ENTITIES IN THE TOMBS

Excavators in Egypt found stone or wooden images in the tombs. They were called ushabti and were placed with the mummy so that they would do all the work for the deceased in the next world. The tomb of King Seti, who lived about 1300 B.C., was said to have 700 of these images in his tomb, all of them considered wooden laborers.

Some tombs were found with portrait images of the deceased These were supposed to be the dwelling place for the ka. Experts are divided on the ka. Some say it represented the dead man's spiritual double. Others maintained that it was a separate entity, or guardian angel. The ka inhabited the spirit world.

When an Egyptian died, he joined one's ka. Today, believers in Egyptian lore believe that if you chant the name ka repeatedly you will get what you ask for in your silent prayers. The ka, however, was not the soul. The soul took the form of a human-headed hawk, call the ba, or ba-soul, or bai. Images of the ba-soul always stood near the mummy. It is said that after a man's death the ba-soul lives mostly in the after-world, but does occasionally visit the mummy in the tomb.

THE WEIRD LIGHT AT THE THIRD PYRAMID

Two men spent a night in the desert near the pyramids. They were Dr. Abbate Pacha, vice president of the Institut Egyptien, and William Groff, a member of the Institut. In the official report of their experience, Groff wrote: "Towards eight o'clock in the evening I noticed a light which appeared to turn slowly around the

THE PYRAMIDS SPEAK

Third Pyramid almost up to the apex. It was like a small flame. The light made three circuits, round the Pyramid and then disappeared. For a good part of the night I attentively watched this Pyramid; towards eleven o'clock I again noticed the same light, but this time it was of a bluish color; it moved slowly almost in a straight line and arrived at a certain height above the Pyramid's summit and then disappeared."

Groff and Dr. Pacha wasted no time questioning Bedouins in the area. All of them gave the men the same answer. The light had been seen at this pyramid for centuries. The Arabs insisted that it was the pyramid's guardian spirit. Groff worked hard to find some natural explanation for what he saw, but finally had to give up. He could find none. Some wise men say the light was the ka of the man buried in the tomb, and that it was destined to appear at that location for eternity.

BLACK MAGIC

The practice of using images in black magic ceremonies undoubtedly began with ancient Egyptians. Ramses III, who reigned about 1200 B.C., discovered that a treasury official used wax dolls in an effort to kill the king. It failed because he was caught in time and exposed as a practitioner in the black arts.

King Nectanebo II (about 350 B.C.) also found black magic to be useful. The legend has it that he fought his battles with wax figures. Whenever real land or sea forces attacked his garrisons, he would animate his wax soldiers and sailors and ships and use them to counterattack the animated enemy forces. He saw to it, of course, that his army always won, and the real counterparts fell dead when the waxen images fell.

Eventually, the gods stepped in. Counteraction was taken against the king; his waxen army lost. Nectanebo took that action as a sign that he had fallen out of favor with the gods. He fled to Greece and became a doctor and magic worker.

BOOKS OF THE DEAD

The Egyptians were undoubtedly the first to use spells and incantations to animate images and work magic in general. The words apparently had intrinsic power. They were known to the gods, priests and magicians. The dead had to know them to complete their journey into the next world. The spells were awesome. Many of them gave mortals the power to command gods or demons.

But it was the dead who really needed this power to make sure the transition to the next world went smoothly. Often, papyri containing sacred words were buried with the dead. These papyri were known as "The Books of the Dead." They were a very large collection of religious and magical hymns, incantations to the gods, spells and formulas to satisfy the wants of the dead. There were chapters on how to conduct a funeral rite. There were special incantations to be given over a picture of the sun-god Ra and his boat. This boat accompanied the deceased so that he might travel with the god forever. Other incantations were spoken to ward off demons, or to give magical powers to objects.

THE RESURRECTION OF OSIRIS AND THE SECRET MYSTERIES

This is the miracle story of the great god Osiris and of his life after death. On earth, Osiris was a beloved king. He had a brother named Set who murdered Osiris, and so furious was his rage that he tore the body into 14 pieces and scattered them along the Nile.

There was great tribulation, especially with Isis, who was Osiris' wife. She was terribly grief-stricken. Somehow, however, she managed to recover all of the pieces of her husband. Using bindings of linen cloth she was able to put the pieces back together again. Isis now called on a god of the netherworld named Anubis. She needed help. She used powerful charms. With those charms and with the help of Anubis, she was able to breathe life into Osiris.

It was not possible for Osiris to return to earth as a man, but he did enter the other world as its ruler, and he became the most powerful god of the dead. Anubis now was the god of preserving the body of the dead for the afterlife, and Isis became the protectress of the dead.

At the time all of this occurred, Isis was pregnant. She gave birth to a son she named Horus. From the time Horus was old enough to understand, he swore vengeance on his father's murder. At last the day came when Horus was strong enough to challenge his uncle Set in battle. The struggle was actually fearful to behold. Both contestants were bloodstained from head to foot. Horus won the fight, but lost his left eye.

Horus then became a beloved god and a protector of mankind His plucked eye became a symbol by which the deceased would see again. It is shown in drawings as the falcon's eye and is called "the eye of Horus." Amulets and charms show this eye and they are necessary in the rites of mummification.

The murder of Osiris is symbolically repeated with every initiate who hopes to learn the secrets of the Mysteries.

THE MYSTERIES

Osiris was the founder of those Mysteries. To become united with the Mysteries, the initiate must allow himself to be "murdered." The initiation is quite scary and is still practiced today by special priests known as hierophants. It is done in any one of the old temples which are divided into two separate rooms; one is for ordinary religion, and the other is for the secret Mysteries. This room is in a special part of the sanctuary and is self-contained. Eavesdroppers would be hard put to intrude on the secret rites.

Candidates are not chosen in a haphazard manner. They must be men of learning and of deep philosophical bent. Almost without exception only Egyptians are selected. However, a few fortunate foreigners were privileged to become initiates—none however, in recent times.

The foreigners were Plato, Pythagoras, Thales, Lycurgus, Solon, Iamblichus, Plutarch and Herodotus. By looking at those names you can deduce that the Egyptians have not found anyone worthy of such an adventure in a very long time.

CANDIDATES EXPERIENCE LIVING DEATH

Of course, nothing is really secret now in Egypt. The Mysteries, in essence, have been revealed, too. And the basic rite is that the candidate is plunged into a deathlike trance.

This is done by the use of powerful fumigants, hypnotism, and a rod magically impregnated. The trance is truly deathlike. There is no breathing, no heart beat, no pulse, no movement, and not even the fluttering of eyelids. The soul is held to the body by only an invisible thread seen by the clairvoyant initiator and no one else.

Despite the complete suspension of animation, the vital functions are preserved. This is the closest anyone can get to death without actually passing over. The purpose of the trance is to teach the initiate that there is no death. The ancients knew that merely telling someone that death does not exist was not enough; it had to be experienced. The initiate therefore experiences dying and being taken into another world.

Finally, the candidate is placed in a mummy-case and the lid is closed and sealed. A modern doctor would pronounce the man dead, and he is for all practical purposes. After a certain length of time, the lid is opened and the candidate is slowly brought back to life. This is roughly what is done during the sacred rites. No one knows exactly what happens, or how long the body remains sealed. The candidate however, is now aware of the resurrection of Osiris in the best way possible—he experienced it himself!

THE EXPERTISE OF THE HIGH PRIESTS

In the early days, many high priests were extraordinarily proficient in hypnotism. Practitioners today can't compare with them. Their knowledge was so great that it was possible for them to place a person in a cataleptic state to such a depth that the rigor mortis of death appeared in the body.

THE PYRAMIDS SPEAK

Further, they were able to keep the candidate's mind awake and thinking clearly even though the body was rigid in pseudo-death. The high priest then guided the man through a series of supernatural experiences, every one of which was remembered by the initiate upon awakening.

PREVIEW OF THE OTHER WORLD

The purpose of the rites was to enlighten candidates to the fact that there was another world after this one, and that the best way to prove it was to show it to them. Scientists know now that the process of enlightenment went far deeper than mere hypnotism. The word is used here and in other texts only as a means of relating what actually happened. There is no word in English, or Egyptian for that matter, to describe the process of living-death.

The preview of the other world was given only to a very few people. The population was simply told that the other world existed and the people were expected to believe it. One candidate declared, "Thanks to the Mysteries, death for mortals is not an evil but a good."

ROMAN SCHOLAR PLUTARCH SPEAKS OF MYSTERIES

Like the other foreigners who were privileged to become initiates, Plutarch was reluctant to reveal everything he saw and felt while in a trance. He did say that there was a psychological purpose of the Mysteries and reported it in his treatise De Iside et Osiride:

"While we are here below, encumbered by bodily affections, we can have no intercourse with God, save as in philosophical thought we may faintly touch Him as in a dream. But when our souls are released by the Mysteries and have passed into the region of the pure, invisible and changeless, this God will be their guide and kind who depend on Him and gaze with insatiable longing on the beauty which may not be spoken of by the lips of man."

PLATO THE PHILOSOPHER

"In consequence of this divine initiation we become spectators of single and blessed visions, resident in a pure light; and were ourselves made immaculate and liberated from this surrounding garment which we call the body and to which we are now bound like an oyster shell."

Plato felt that the purpose of the Mysteries was to return men to the principles from which the race had originally fell.

MOSES—THE MOST FAMOUS FREEMASON INITIATE

Moses was half Hebrew, half Egyptian. The New Testament says, "Moses was instructed in all the wisdom of the Egyptians." What that statement means is that the deepest wisdoms were open to him. He had a knowledge of the Mysteries and was truly an initiate. If you search the Scriptures you will find a passage reading: "Moses put a veil upon his face." It doesn't mean that he used a cloth to cover his face, but was a pledge to remain silent about his initiation into the Mysteries. In Corinthians, 2nd Epistle you will find these words: "...until this very day at the reading of the Old Testament the same veil remaineth unlifted."

MOSES THE ADEPT

Moses learned his wisdom in the famous temple school in the city of On. It is called On in the Bible, but when the Greeks conquered Egypt they renamed the city Heliopolis. It stood a few miles north of Cairo.

Heliopolis was a great center of learning, sacred and secular. There were 13,000 priest-students and teachers in the city and the population was enormous. The library at Heliopolis helped form the famous Alexandrian one. Moses was a serious child. He studied hard, poring over his rolls of papyri as he strolled around the temples. Nor did he have trouble with his initiation degrees, reaching that rare position of an Adept. His next step was to become a hierophant. He attained this distinction in the school attached to the Great Temple of Heliopolis, the City of the Sun. And, of course, as a hierophant he was asked to receive candidates into the secret rites of Osiris, which was the highest rites of the Mysteries.

MOSES—NOT HIS REAL NAME

The original name of the great leader was an Egyptian one, Osarsiph. The ancient Egyptian records of a priest named Manetho reveals the true name. It was not until a great change came into the life of Moses that he selected the Hebrew name. The choice was not haphazard one. All Egyptian scholars believed in the power of names; it had a magical power, this one that Moses took, just as other names did for other Adepts and hierophants.

MOSES BREAKS WITH THE PHARAOH

The Pharaoh in the time of Moses was cruel and stubborn. Moses, being half Hebrew, was outraged by the harsh treatment of the Israrelites in Egypt. He sympathized with the persecuted people to such an extent that he succeeded in freeing the Hebrew tribes from their captivity. He took them out of the valley of Goshen and along the old historic highway which was the road between Africa and Asia.

THE PENTATEUCHT AND MISINTERPRETATIONS

The series of books in the Old Testament called the Pentateuch are attributed to Moses. These books are gold mines of information about the wisdom Moses wished to impart to his people, historical facts about the creation of the world, and the early races of man. Unfortunately, Moses wrote them in Egyptian hieroglyphs.

THE PYRAMIDS SPEAK

Only initiated priests could understand them.

As time passed, matters grew worse. By the fourth century A.D. the art of deciphering hieroglyphs was completely lost, even in Egypt. The Israelites settled in Palestine and more centuries passed before Moses' hieroglyphs were tackled. Priests found themselves struggling with the strange signs and symbols.

Once in awhile a meaning would become clear, but for the most part the job of reading hieroglyphs was like breaking a secret code. One thousand years after the great exodus of the Israelites from Egypt, Israelite elders put together a collection of books we call the Old Testament. Moses' writings were almost impossible to translate. Moses wrote as an Adept. The elders were certainly scholarly, but they were not Adepts.

As a result, there were many misunderstandings. Symbolic expressions were taken literally. Hieroglyphic pictures were thought to be the pictures of things that really happened. Figurative phrases were misinterpreted. For instance, the six days' of creation did not mean that at all. Moses meant that there were vast periods of time involved in the creation, but in his writings the periods were designated as days. Adepts knew what he meant. But the scholars who translated him were sure he meant days as in twenty-four hour periods.

This explains why the Old Testament is replete with peculiar notions when read literally. Today, science is working to correct the errors made by translators.

EGYPT, ATLANTIS AND ANCIENT ASTRONAUTS

There is a mystery about Egypt which has never been solved to anyone's satisfaction. It is the sudden blossoming of civilization. Researchers know that around 3100 B.C. the Egyptians were a primitive people. They lived in small homes made of sun-dried brick or adobe. They were slightly better off than the cavemen who preceded them.

The space shuttle Columbia showed in November 1981 that the remains of the Stone Age still exist in southwestern Egypt and northwestern Sudan. The shuttle's radar penetrated to a depth of 16 feet and picked up axe heads, spears, arrow tips and corn-grinding tools. That equipment had been there for 40,000 years.

The point is that quite suddenly, around 3000 B.C. and only 100 years after the Egyptians were considered primitive, there was advanced civilization in that country. The first pyramid, at Sakkara, was built. It was a step" or "false" pyramid, so-called because it did not have smooth sides. Imhotep was the architect. He was considered a man of many sciences. How did he gather so many talents when there were no masters available at that time?

During that same period, the first pharaoh, Narmer-Mena, brought with him a

THE PYRAMIDS SPEAK

flourishing political life, philosophy, religion and military might. How did this happen so abruptly when only a century earlier there is no record anywhere of the Egyptians being anything but primitive? There is no trace of civilization in Egypt before 3000 B.C.

Think about it. Think how long it took for us to reach our level of civilization, then compare it with the Egyptians' burgeoning growth. What's the answer? Did they have help from somewhere else?

THE MYSTERY OF TOOLS

When the first pyramid at Sakkara was built, the tools and the architectural technique had to come from somewhere else. Neither existed in Egypt at that time. It is also quite odd to note that this "step" pyramid is almost a duplicate of the kind that were built in Mexico, thousands of miles away.

The Great Pyramid of Cheops, built around 2900 B.C. or 2800 B.C., was an architectural marvel. It certainly wasn't improvised as it went along. The pyramid was constructed only after great care was taken. The specifications and preparations had taken years. Suddenly, there were all sorts of metal tools and machinery to erect the huge monument. A knowledge of chemistry was apparent because of the cement that was mixed and used as mortar, paper thin, between the precision-carved stones.

The location of the Great Pyramid indicates beyond a doubt that the builders had a thorough knowledge of astronomy. The pyramid is not only oriented toward the North Star, but is also oriented toward the Polar axis. That feat requires precise calculations based on accurate geodesic knowledge as well as astronomy. How did these so-called ignorant Egyptians suddenly attain so much knowledge? Were they inspired by God? Did members of a super race, now extinct, visit them? Did they have help from visitors from another planet?

A STRANGE TALE

A demotic script was found in the artifacts in the tomb of a feudal lord. Demotic writing was a simplified form of Egyptian hieroglyphics. The tale told here indicates that it was written at about the time the first three pyramids were built. The locale is vague. It could have taken place near the outlet of the Red Sea, or in the Indian Ocean, in the Atlantic or the Mediterranean.

The story reveals how a sailor survived a shipwreck and reached a land where there were fruit trees in abundance and vast areas of sweet vegetables. The men who lived on this land were extremely wise. The story says that the land sank beneath the sea and everyone on it fled in all directions. Many of them found a haven in Egypt.

THE PYRAMIDS SPEAK

The story writer suggested that the land was near the coast of Africa. Could this have been the lost continent of Atlantis? Scholars have studied this demotic script for years and some say the story is fantasy, others are convinced it is a reality.

ANOTHER SOURCE

An Egyptian priest of Neith Sais spoke at length of the sunken continent to an Athenian statesman and lawgiver named Solon, who passed the story on to his son, Critias the elder. He told it to Critias the younger, who then repeated it to Plato. The brief narrative appeared in Plato's Dialogues called Critias and Timaceus.

True? No one knows for sure. But one thing we do know is that India is presently investigating the bottom of the Indian Ocean. The tableland here indicates that it was once above sea level and was inhabited by people. There are traces of temple ruins belonging to a lost civilization.

About ten years ago it was reported that the alleged remains of the famous city of Poseidon were found opposite the Straits of Gibraltar. To the ancients of the Mediterranean the Straits were known as the Pillars of Hercules. Their ' history tells us that they knew about the sunken city and said it was at the exact point where the place was recently discovered. Investigations by the Spanish government reveal that a ruined city does exist on the bottom of the Atlantic Ocean near the Straits.

Did the continent of Atlantis really exist? Nearly 20 years ago this news item appeared in papers around the world: "Athens, Greece, September 3, 1966 (AP). Greek professor and seismologist Angelos Galanopoulus stated today that he and a group of North American scientists have found traces in the Aegean Sea of what could be legendary Atlantis.

"Galanopoulus, working with scientists from the Institute of Oceanography, Woods Hole, Mass., said the finds were made near the island of Santorini (Thera) at no great depth.

"Galanopoulus stated that Atlantis sank because of a tremendous volcanic eruption. The use of the hydrographic boat Chain enabled the explorers to locate a submarine trench similar to the moat which, according to Plato, surrounded the principal city of Atlantis. He noted that the tremendous eruption that destroyed Atlantis caused waves three hundred and fifty times more powerful than a hydrogen bomb, and that the catastrophe also destroyed Knossus, capital of the Minoan civilization in Crete."

Explorations here turned up evidence of a very advanced civilization. Discoveries included ceramics, docks, breakwaters and other artifacts.

POSSIBLE ANSWER TO EGYPT'S INSTANT CULTURE

Let's assume that the people of Atlantis did reach a high level of culture before the great catastrophe struck. Their instincts during the danger would be to conserve the knowledge it took them centuries to develop. So it is reasonable to suggest that those who made it safely to Egypt immediately began rebuilding their civilization.

But what did they have to work with? The people of Egypt were primitive. The newcomers needed manpower for labor forces. They also needed to train those who appeared capable of learning. The job of restoring their lost heritage was incredibly difficult. And the fact is that the people of the lost continent may have even failed in their tasks.

Certainly, there was compromise. Their original plans must have been altered to suit the abilities of the Egyptians. But despite these problems, the Egyptians, within 100 years, became cultured and civilized. One wonders how far advanced they would have been if more people from Atlantis had come to the Land of the Nile, or if the Egyptians would have been more receptive to knowledge than they had been.

So one theory holds that the sudden rise in Egyptian civilization was the direct result of the work of Atlanteans trying to preserve their own dead culture. But there is still another theory.

DID ANCIENT ASTRONAUTS VISIT EGYPT?

Not too long ago it was considered too incredible to think that visitors from outer space arrived in Egypt during the period of 3100 B.C. and 3000 B.C. That's not the case now. Our own experiments in space travel have convinced many scholars that the old theory may be true. One of them is Professor Agreste, a University of Moscow mathematician, who feels that at one time there were visitors from outer space who came to earth regularly.

The professor says that in the first books of the Bible, written by Hebrew priests, there is a story about beings coming from the sky who, like Enoch, appeared and vanished on arcs of intense, blinding lights. Professor Agreste also has more concrete evidence of space visitations. While traveling with his wife through the desert region around Baalbek (ancient Heliopolis, Lebanon), he found pieces of glass, or objects that look like glass.

He gathered them up and sent them to a laboratory for analysis. He learned that they were tiny meteorites from space, originally radioactive isotopes of beryl and aluminum. Actually, they were artificially produced nuclear particles which were definitely not of earthly origin.'

There are several reports in ancient Hindu literature describing spacecraft. The following is one of them: "Kukra, flying aboard a high-powered Vimana, fired on the triple city a single projectile loaded with the force of the universe. A great incandescent cloud of smoke took on the splendor of a thousand suns. When the Vimana landed, it looked like a beautiful block of antimony resting on the earth." This description certainly suggests that not only were there spacecraft in those days, but also nuclear explosions.

ANCIENT NUCLEAR AGE

The Old Testament tradition insists that there were so-called cities of the damned in the Dead Sea area. Professor Agreste goes along with that belief because in his explorations of the Dead Sea area he has found abundant evidence to prove that space ships once landed there.

The professor's theory is that ancient aliens from some other world brought atomic fuels to this planet, and that when they decided to abandon earth they destroyed the atomic fuels before they became a danger to the people.

Cities in the Dead Sea area were told that evacuation was necessary to avoid the dangers of nuclear explosion and radioactive fallout. In most cases the warnings were ignored, just as they were at Hiroshima and Nagasaki. The nuclear blasts came and the people were destroyed.

The destruction of Sodom and Gomorrah has puzzled scholars for centuries. The question is: what sort of combustible element could cause such a disaster? Perhaps we now know. The Dead Sea Scrolls have enlightened us in some areas of history in the thousand years before Christ. They don't shed any light on the fate of Sodom, but they do tell us something quite interesting about spacecraft. One passage reads:

"The beings who came from the sky were living on earth in those times and afterwards, when the fallen sons of God arrived..."

THE HINDUS AND UFOS

In two ancient Hindu books, the Ramayana and the Mahabarata, both more than 3,000 years old, there are descriptions of UFOs. They describe Vimanas (spacecraft) as circling the heavens at the beginning of time. The writers said the ships looked like blue egg-shaped clouds.

According to Hindu accounts, the spacecraft took off from earth with a great deal of vibration. Sweet musical sounds were heard from the ships. They glowed

THE PYRAMIDS SPEAK

like fire and spun slowly, alternately swooping down to earth and then leaping back up into space. An inscription in the Purva mausoleum in India read: "It was an unknown weapon, a gigantic iron ray, a messenger of death that reduced to ashes all members of the Vrishni and Andhaka races. Their bodies were burned beyond recognition. Their hair and nails fell out. Clay objects broke with no apparent cause. Birds turned white. At the end of several hours, all food was spoiled. The ray disintegrated into fine dust." There can be no doubt that the destruction here was caused by a nuclear explosion.

THE BOOK OF DZYAN AND UFOS

This Tibetan book tells about men with shining faces who abandoned the earth. They took all of their knowledge with them rather than leave it to the people on earth who were still too primitive to appreciate it. All traces of their life on this planet were erased. They left in flying cars that were moved by light.

STRANGE DESCRIPTION FOUND IN THE POPUL VUH

When you read the ancient texts of various countries you realize that Egypt was not the only land favored by aliens from other worlds. In the Popol Vuh, the sacred book of the Quiche Mayans of southern Mexico and Guatemala, there is a passage which reads (the first men were)... "endowed with intelligence. They looked and instantly they saw into the distance, they succeeded in seeing and knowing all that there is in the world. When they looked, they saw on all sides, and they observed the arch of heaven and the round face of earth in turn. Things hidden in the distance they could see without moving. Their wisdom was great; their sight penetrated the forests, the rocks, the lakes, the seas, the mountains and valleys."

These "first people" obviously had equipment which was strong enough to see things at great distances, similar to our television sets. They saw the earth as a "round face," indicating they must have seen it from outer space. Interestingly, it was in Mexico that pyramids not unlike those in Egypt were found. Did the same aliens who visited Egypt also visit Mexico?

PORTRAIT OF A SPACE VISITOR

Explorer Henry Lothe poked around the Hoggar Plateau in Sahara Desert and discovered buildings and columns that were extraordinarily tall. He went into the town of Jabbaren nearby. The place is also known as the City of Giants, and it was here that he found prehistoric paintings which were done in a style completely different from anything found elsewhere in the world.

While probing one of the caves in the area, Lothe found a painted figure on the wall. It was three yards high and showed a man wearing a transparent visor-helmet much like the type worn today by astronauts. The helmet was round. Many of the investigators who saw it after Lothe are agreed that the ancient artist tried to portray a visitor from another world. Lothe named the figure "The Martian." Later, other Martian-like figures were found, although there is no evidence as to where the models came from.

One interesting note, however, is that all of the painted figures are estimated to be 10,000 years old! That discovery is not unique. You can see rock paintings showing figures with helmets, and with antennae emitting sparks, in the Tassili caves of the Sahara Desert. Others can be seen in Akka, Moghar, Tibesti, Ennedi, Air and Timisao.

Explorers in the Gobi Desert found vitrified soil. This is a phenomenon produced by atomic explosions. The Gobi Desert, and also Turkestan, have produced some strange looking ceramic or glass objects with a drop of mercury in the end. These were found in caves. In the caves of Bohistan there were astronomical maps and inscriptions painted on rocks. They showed the constellations in positions they occupied five thousand years ago. Some of the lines connected Venus and earth, as though marking a route.

Explorers in those regions never really know what they will turn up. Even a visit to one of the older museums in the near east can sometimes produce amazing results. Explorer William went to the Baghdad museum as a tourist and spotted some flat stones that had been found in Iraq. He suspected they weren't stones at all, and upon close examination he learned they were actually electric cells that had been manufactured more than two thousand years ago.

According to the legends of the Inca Indians, white men came out of the sky and ruled over them for thousands of years. The atmospheric pressure on the high plateaus of Peru and Bolivia is very low, yet tribes find no difficulty in living and working in that area. Carbon 14 tests revealed that the region has been inhabited by humans for thirty thousand years.

If you were to view the Nasca Plains of Peru from the air you would see geometrical lines and totem-like figures of birds and animals traced on the barren landscape. The lines were obviously made by humans. Some are parallel; some crisscross each other. They extend for hundreds of yards and it would be impossible for anyone to do it without the aid of aircraft.

The figures of the birds and animals are so large they can only be identified from the air. There are no nearby high peaks from which men might have guided the artists. Did the figures act as guides or identification markers, or symbols for spacecraft coming into earth's atmosphere? No one knows. The real tragedy is that we may never find out.

THE PYRAMIDS SPEAK

THE GATE OF THE SUN

One of the most amazing monuments in the world is the colossal Gateway of the Sun. It is located on the shores of Lake Titicaca in the Peruvian Andes. Carved into the stone is the most ancient calendar in the world. The estimate is that the calendar is between 12,000 and 15,000 years old.

The most incredible part of it all is that it is not a calendar of the earth year, but is one based on the Venusian year! Carved into the stone is the time it takes Venus to make one complete orbit around the sun. Its two hundred and twenty-five days are divided into fifty-five day months. The planet Venus has been associated with the white god Quetzalcoatl, who returned to the heavens after a long reign on earth.

One wonders why the ancient Peruvians would be concerned with the calendar year of another planet. Even more baffling is how they were so accurate in their calculations when they had no knowledge of astronomy and no telescopes to scan the heavens.

All of what we have said here is circumstantial evidence. We don't know for sure that aliens from other worlds visited this planet in ancient times. What we do know is that there is a unique sameness concerning the old legends. Apparently, no matter where the legends materialize—Egypt, Mexico, Peru, the Sahara—the stories are similar enough to cause one to wonder. Certainly, there could have been no communications among the people of these regions. Ocean travel was not possible. There were no conveyances for overland treks.

That leaves a common denominator. Someone, or a group of beings, must have had the ability to touch all of these primitive people at various periods in history. From this vantage point the only answer is: Ancient astronauts .

DOES A TIME CAPSULE EXIST UNDER A PYRAMID?

Two famed psychics who lived in different centuries stated that important information lies buried under the Sphinx and one the pyramids in Giza.

Edgar Cayce was one of the psychics. Cayce was able to go into a trance and diagnose any disease without medical training. Before World War I started he had a vision of a huge fleet of airships passing overhead. He dropped to his knees and prayed. Soon after, the war started. In the files of the Association for Research and Enlightenment is a document written by Cayce which says that "if the Versailles Conference succeeded, the world would experience a millennium of peace and prosperity. If it failed, the world would see the same elements plunging humanity into a second and far more terrible war by 1940."

Cayce also predicted the Wall Street Crash, the Depression, the independence of India, Hitler's defeat and the rise of the Soviet Union.

According to Cayce, a time capsule is buried in Egypt in a sealed vault. It contains all of the historical records of Atlantis. He wrote that the secret underground chamber's location was "as the sun rises from the waters—as the line of the shadow (or light) falls between the paws of the Sphinx."

Cayce said that the storehouse contained records, tablets and documents of Atlantean and early Egyptian origin. There are mummies, gold and precious stones, surgical instruments and a complete record of how the pyramids were built. The psychic said that the great structures went up by means of levitating the huge stone blocks.

The idea of levitation was also suggested by an authority on Egypt named Desmond Leslie, whose theory was that since many of the stones weighed three tons, it was impossible for the Egyptians to get them into place with their crude equipment. Leslie also stated that each stone in the pyramids was 1/100ths of an inch from its neighbors, and to achieve such precision, levitation had to be employed.

CAYCE SAW RISE OF ATLANTIS

Cayce was called "The Sleeping Prophet" because his predictions were accomplished while he was in a trance. Over the years he predicted that there would be a great catastrophe between 1958 and 1998. Reason: Shifting of the poles. He said that during this cataclysm there would be volcanic eruptions so powerful that land would appear in the Atlantic and Pacific Oceans. San Francisco and Los Angeles would likely be destroyed. New York City would also be ruined.

The Great Lakes will empty into the Gulf of Mexico instead of the Atlantic. Presumably, the land mass between those two great bodies of water would be flooded. Cayce saw new lands rising in the Caribbean, and the contours of northern Europe would be changed. The north and south poles will suffer upheavals. South America will be shaken. Japan will sink into the sea.

The prophet said these changes would be gradual and there would be ample warnings. The rise of Atlantis, when it comes, will make archaeologists very happy because they will find a temple on the new land and it will contain the records of a lost race.

CHEIRO'S PROPHECY

When Edgar Cayce was just beginning his career as a psychic, Count Louis de Hamon (Cheiro) was winding his down. Count Louis de Hamon dabbled in the medieval arts of chiromancy, astrology and Cabbala at the close of the last century. He was so good at it that he attracted the attention of royalty and celebrities.

THE PYRAMIDS SPEAK

The Count was born in Ireland. He was able to trace his Norman ancestry back to Rollo, the first Duke of Normandy. When he began his studies of the occult sciences, he called himself Cheiro.

Was he good at prophecy? Judge for yourself. In 1894 he warned Lord Kitchener that he would be involved in a disaster at sea in his 66th year. This prediction was the result of an astrology reading. The British general kept the horoscope with him at all times, even when he died aboard the Hampshire in 1916. He was 66 years old.

Early in 1900 Cheiro was asked by the King of Italy to make a forecast. Cheiro did. It predicted that King Humbert would die within three months. In July 1900 the king was assassinated at Monza.

Cheiro predicted the Boer War (1899-1902), World War I, which he said, rightly that it would last four years, and the independence of Ireland and India.

CHEIRO'S PREDICTION ABOUT THE GREAT PYRAMID

Cheiro said that a great archaeological discovery would be made under the Great Pyramid at Giza:

"Beneath the thirteen acre base of the pyramid a treasure temple will be discovered, one not only containing gold and jewels beyond the wildest dreams of legislation, but revealing scientific secrets by which the pyramid was built, which will upset all previously known laws relating to astronomy, gravitation, electricity, the harnessing of the powers of light, etheric rays and the hidden forces of the atom."

His following prophecy was similar to Cayce's. Cheiro said that there would be sudden geological catastrophes which would be felt everywhere on earth. New land would appear in the Atlantic Ocean. This would alter the course of the Gulf Stream, which in turn would change the climate of the Northern Hemisphere. Cheiro said that when the submerged continent of Atlantis finally rose out of its depths, there would be tidal waves, volcanoes and earthquakes.

ANCIENT MYSTERIES

How did the world look in 9000 B.C.? Geologists tell us that Scandinavia was still a glacial wilderness. Most of Europe was uninhabitable. Neolithic man in the Mediterranean area was beginning to learn how to sharpen stone tools. At about 8000 B.C. lake dwellings built on pilings appeared in Central Europe. Villages in Mesopotamia were built of adobe, wheat was cultivated, and livestock was raised.

Does this civilization sound capable of understanding the stars and devising a zodiac? Of course not. Yet, that is exactly what happened. If you went to the

THE PYRAMIDS SPEAK

Biblioteque National in Paris you would see the huge zodiac carved on an enormous stone. It was taken from the ceiling of the temple of Hathor at Dendera, on the banks of the Nile. Starting with the sign of Leo at the spring equinox, the Zodiac indicates a cycle of 9,000 years or more before the birth of Christ.

Pyramidologists say that a man could spend his whole life studying the Great Pyramid without exhausting the mystic and scientific aspects of the structure. The same can be said of the Dendera Zodiac. It's said that the Zodiac of Dendera was carved in the land where it was quarried, but that land is unknown to students of geology and archaeology. The Zodiac shows the signs in an order indicating a time nine thousand years before Christ, when the constellations occupied different positions in the sky from those they do now.

Oddly enough, Plato mentions the year 9000 B.C. as the time Atlantis disappeared into the ocean. We know that nine thousand years before Christ the Egyptians were no more advanced culturally than any other people. It was not at all likely that they carved the Zodiac. However, if the Atlanteans had swept into Egypt after the sinking of their continent, there would be an answer to the strange mystery.

WHO INVENTED ASTROLOGY?

The Mesopotamians are credited with inventing astrology at about 2000 B.C. Undoubtedly, they must have been star gazing for thousands of years before that. But who studied the heavens in 9000 B.C.? Archeological evidence indicates that man was neolithic* even 4,000 years before Christ. The date 4000 B.C. is traditionally assigned to Adam's appearance on earth.

* The **Neolithic** Era, or Period, or **New Stone age**, was a period in the development of human technology, beginning about 10,200 BC in some parts of the Middle East, and later in other parts of the world, and ending between 4,500 and 2,000 BC.

Traditionally considered the last part of the Stone Age, the Neolithic followed the terminal Holocene Epipaleolithic period and commenced with the beginning of farming, which produced the "Neolithic Revolution". It ended when metal tools became widespread (in the Copper Age or Bronze Age; or, in some geographical regions, in the Iron Age). The Neolithic is a progression of behavioral and cultural characteristics and changes, including the use of wild and domestic crops and of domesticated animals.

Then there is the matter of tools. When the Zodiac of Dendera was carved there were no tools intricate enough to create the precision that went into the carving of the Zodiac.

THE PYRAMIDS SPEAK

THE AZTEC CALENDAR WAS CARVED WITHOUT TOOLS

This is the big argument of historians. The Stone of the Sun, which is the Aztec Calendar, is 12 feet in diameter and was carved without tools. These people, too, were well-versed in astronomy and in the history of the earth in past eons. It records four cataclysms and predicts a fifth. The Aztec Calendar, however, was carved only four or five hundred years ago.

WHERE DO THE ANCIENT ZODIACS ORIGINATE?

The Stone of the Sun does not help to explain where the Zodiac of Dendera originated. Nor does any branch of research. No one has been able to discover facts which would reveal how the Zodiac of Dendera came into being. The answer, apparently, lies at the bottom of the Atlantic Ocean. Common sense tells us that either the highly cultured Atlanteans constructed the Zodiac of Dendera, or it was done by visitors from another world. We tend to think that if space aliens made the Zodiac they would have used a more sophisticated material. Also, if they were responsible, it is likely they would have destroyed it along with all of the other evidence of their visit to this planet.

A STRANGE KINSHIP

Another mystery exists. It may never be explained. It is the fact that the architecture of Egypt is similar to that of Mexico. Also similar is the folklore of both peoples. Religious rites and myths are incredibly alike.

We have already noted the similarity of the pyramids. Historians Yban Ayas and Macrizy of 1100 A.D. wrote that the agrarian festivals they witnessed in Egypt were vestiges of ancient religious rites culminating in the sacrifice of a beautiful girl by drowning her in the Nile to placate the river god in serpentine form and to make the land fertile.

Historians in Mexico describe the same kind of sacrifice and for the same reasons in Chichen Itza. In the Yucatan, Mexico, Mayan girls were thrown into a sacred well called a cenote. In Mexico and in Egypt, the girls were dressed in finery and adorned with jewels. The sacrifice always took place in public. If the girl survived in Yucatan, it meant the god had rejected the offering, and that meant that crops would fail and there would be hunger among the people. Like the Nile god, the god of the river in Yucatan also took the shape of a snakes

Coincidence? Not likely. There must have been a common denominator. Were Atlanteans capable of crossing oceans to spread their religious rites and ceremonies? The answer will come only when the lost continent is found.

THE PYRAMIDS SPEAK

UNCANNY COINCIDENCE BETWEEN OSIRIS AND CHRIST

Ancient Egyptian texts refer to the Grand Gallery in the Great Pyramid as representing the epoch of the savior of the human race. It is the passion of the Messiah and the crossing of the pure waters of life. The writers were talking about their god Osiris. They could have been reporting on the birth and death of Jesus Christ. In fact, Christ's life on earth is clearly defined in the Great Pyramid's chronological system, the birth being level with the floor of the horizontal passage and the death being on the second level with its roof. The distance between these two points, worked out mathematically, runs from Jesus' birth in 4 B.C. to His death in 30 A.D.

WAS JESUS A REINCARNATION OF THE EGYPTIAN GOD OSIRIS?

The author of "The Gods and Kings of Egypt," Alexander Moret, tells us that long before the arrival of the Hebrews in Egypt, the mythology in the land of the Nile spoke of a Messiah. The incredible aspect of this is that they spoke of it in nearly the same words that are found in the Old and New Testaments! In ancient Egyptian traditions, according to Moret, you can find the details of the passion in the Last Supper. There was nothing secret about these teachings in hermetic schools; it was lore well known through public rites. Ironically, the teachings referred not to Jesus, but to the god of their own past, Osiris. Can we gather from this that Christianity is a revival of the beliefs held by the pharaohs?

The next question is even more intriguing: ***Was Jesus the reincarnation of Osiris?***

THE RECORD OF HUMAN HISTORY

It's evident that the pyramid builders wanted to make sure that we understood that human history has a set direction which cannot be altered. It is programmed. We can see that in the prophecies of the Great Pyramid, in which historical events were laid out 4,000 years before they occurred.

GREAT PYRAMID RECORDS ACTUAL DATE OF CHRIST'S BIRTH

We celebrate Jesus' birth on December 25th, but it is not the true date. In ancient Greece, this was the birthday of the gods. It was also the birth of the unconquered sun in Rome—the Natalis Solis Invicti. The date was actually an annual pagan festival, falling close to the winter solstice.

Early Christians celebrated Christ's birth, epiphany, and baptism on January 6th. The date wasn't changed until the fourth century A.D., when it became December 25th. On that day all trials, lawsuits, tortures and executions were suspended. If the Romans were at war, they stopped fighting on that day. Wine flowed. Tables were heavy with food. Orgies were not prohibited. The emphasis was on fun rather than religion, and in that respect there has been little change in how we view the holiday today.

Both dates are wrong. Egyptologists have followed the information in the Gospels and, by confirming the date found in the Great Pyramid, have concluded mathematically that Jesus was born on October 5, in the year 4 B.C., on the Feast of Tabernacles, or 5 Tishri.

The details will be explained as we go along.

MYSTERY OF THE STAR OF BETHLEHEM

Astronomers have always been puzzled by the Star of Bethlehem. Their attempts to call it a meteor or comet have failed. Meteors are sighted quite often, even in the daytime, but there is no pattern to their appearances and it is impossible to determine if one was seen in the sky over Near and Middle Eastern countries on the night Christ was born.

The educated thought for a while was that the Star of Bethlehem was really Halley's Comet. Very few comets are visible even with telescopes, although Halley's can be seen with the naked eye. The only problem here is that Halley's Comet was sighted by people in the year 11 B.C. Since this comet makes an appearance every 77 years, there is no possible way it could have been seen in the year 4 B.C.

Some researchers say that the light seen in the sky was Wolf's comet. But this one is not easily sighted. It is not likely that it would have made any impression on anyone looking up. Perhaps the Star of Bethlehem was a nova. Some astronomers seem to think so. These stars flare up brilliantly and then vanish. They are old stars that flare up for some reason and then fade. There are supernovas whose brightness is 10 times that of the sun, but they are so far from earth that they are hardly visible.

ONLY THE WISE MEN SAW THE STAR

In the second chapter of Matthew, verses 1 to 8, we find a clue that the Star was not seen by anyone except the Magi:

Now when Jesus was born in Bethlehem of Judea in the days of Herod the King, behold, certain wise men from the East came to Jerusalem, saying, "Where is he who has been born king of the Jews? For we have seen his star in the East and have come to worship him." And when Herod the king heard this, he was troubled, and all Jerusalem with him. And assembling all the chief priests and scribes of the people, he inquired of them where the Christ was to be born. And they told him, "In Bethlehem of Judea, for it is so written by the prophet. Then Herod summoned the wise men secretly and learned from them what time the star appeared. And he sent them to Bethlehem, saying, "Go and search diligently for the child, and when you have found him, bring me word, that I too may come and worship him."

At a time when unusual signs in the sky stirred fear among the people, there was no such tribulation. There were prophets and astrologers who always searched the skies, yet on that night no one saw the Star of Bethlehem. Herod heard about the star only when the three Oriental visitors told him about it. If the star were a nova, it would have been bright enough for all to see. Many observers would have also seen a comet or a meteor. So why, apparently, did only the three wise men see it?

WERE THE THREE WISE MEN EGYPTIANS?

Not likely. The probability is that they were from Persia The Magi had founded famous schools of occultism that attracted scholars from other countries. One of the wise men may have been Arabian because myrrh, his gift to the Christ Child, is an aromatic gum resin taken from a genus of trees or shrubs found only in Arabia.

They were astrologers, of course. And they were followers of Zoroaster, the Persian prophet of the sixth century B.C. who taught a creed that was essentially monotheistic, or the notion of there being only one God. It is not impossible that the other two wise men were Egyptians; it is simply that no one knows for sure.

WAS THE STAR OF BETHLEHEM A UFO?

If we can believe what we read in the Gospels, then this is the only explanation which makes sense. If you read verses 8-10 of the second chapter of the Gospel according to St. Matthew you will be given pause to wonder. They read: And he sent them to Bethlehem, saying, "Go and search diligently for the child, and when you have found him, bring me word, that I, too, may come and worship him." And when they had heard the words of the king, they went their way; and lo, the star which they had seen in the East went before them, till it came to rest over the place where the child was. And when they saw the star they rejoiced exceedingly.

Astronomers say that it is impossible for any kind of heavenly body to act in such a way. A movement like the one described in the Gospel suggests a flying object, one that is controlled by an intelligence. And because of its shining quality, it looked like a star.

The Gospel tells us of another event which might also be construed as the landing of a UFO. You can read it in Chapter 2, verses 8-10, according to St. Luke: And in that region there were shepherds in the fields, keeping watch over their flocks by night. And an angel of the Lord appeared to them, and the glory of the Lord shone around them, and they were filled with fear. And the angel said to them,

THE PYRAMIDS SPEAK

"Fear not, behold, I bring you tidings of great joy which will come to all people..."

UFOlogists and other researchers interpret this passage as one in which a UFO landed in the field with its great illumination shining over the field. The shepherds were undoubtedly in a state of panic. The alien who alighted from the ship was not dressed like anyone the shepherds had ever seen, so it was assumed he was an angel—especially when you consider that the light shining on him from the ship gave him an eerie glow. Perhaps he was a messenger from God, but not the kind shown in Egyptian and Babylonian paintings, carrying feathered wings on his back.

THE LINK BETWEEN CHRIST, ASTROLOGY AND THE EGYPTIANS

We call the study of astral influences on human life astrology. The influences are exercised by the planets, the sun, and the moon. The sky has been divided into twelve equal parts, or houses, which make up the Zodiac. Planetary influences on a person's birth, a nation's birth, or an organizations's birth are determined by the house in which the planets, the sun and the moon are found at the exact time of the event.

At the time of the ancient astrologers, seven astral bodies were known: Mercury, Venus, Mars, Jupiter, and Saturn, plus the sun and the moon. Calculations concerning the present and future events were based on the position of those seven bodies at that time.

What we know about the three wise men is that they were well versed in astrology. They knew the stellar bodies. They knew their habits, knew their different rates of speed and changing positions. What's more, they knew how to interpret the influences through psychic insight.

This knowledge alone made them wise, but they were also quite familiar with the Messianic prophecies of the Egyptians and the Jews. They knew that those two peoples had predicted the birth of a savior under the sign of Pisces, known as the House of the Jews. And, as you know, Pisces the fish later became a Christian symbol and an anagram for the name of Jesus.

The three wise men perhaps did not see the Star of Bethlehem, but rather a heavy concentration of planets in the house of Pisces. If so, they could have deduced that the Egyptian prophecy concerning the birth of a Messiah was about to be fulfilled.

M. KEPLER, THE MAN WHO PROVED IT

In 1604 M. Kepler observed the conjunction of Jupiter and Saturn (every 20 years Jupiter passes Saturn). That same year he observed the nova. And that year he saw that Mars was in conjunction with those two planets. Kepler's calculations told him that this trio of Mars, Jupiter and Saturn met every 805 years. Carrying that figure backward in time, it was clear that a rendezvous took place among the trio in the year 6 B.C., and the conjunction took place in Pisces.

Does this place the Egyptian prediction that Christ would be born in 4 B.C. off by two years? Not really. Kepler's information was accurate, but not complete. Astronomers who came later showed that a conjunction of those planets occurred in the house of Pisces on May 29, September 29, and December 4, of the year 7 B.C., and also during the summer of 6 B.C.

On December 7, 6 B.C., a great surprise appeared in the sky. At daybreak, the three planets in conjunction passed Venus in the east. If that event happened today, there would be headlines all over the world. TV news programs would devote whole programs to the conjunction. Every amateur astronomer would have his telescope trained on the skies. It can be guessed that there was excitement when the ancients became aware of it.

THE MYSTERY IS NOT SOLVED

The wise men made a journey from Persia, across Mesopotamia and the Syrian Desert. The distance is 1,700 kilometers. It could have been done in just under a year, on camel. If the Magi sighted the conjunction of Jupiter and Saturn in the house of Pisces in 7 B.C., they would have undoubtedly made ready for their trip to Palestine.

If they had made it to Jerusalem in time to see the Venus conjunction, they would have been two years ahead of time. Did they then inform Herod of an event that was coming soon? Or was the Gospel wrong? Obviously, the mystery of when the Star of Bethlehem appeared is still hazy, shrouded in a time period when written communication was at an absolute minimum.

The Great Pyramid tells us that the great day occurred in 4 B.C., but astronomers agree that more data is needed to confirm it. And they have to know exactly what it was that prompted the three Magi to leave their homes to take on a trek of 1,700 kilometers.

WHICH PYRAMID HOLDS THE ARK OF THE COVENANT?

The Ark of the Covenant was kept in the Holiest of the Holies, occupied its chief place of honor and was never to be looked on by anyone other than the High Priest, even during a journey.

The original name, arca, implies that it was a box or a chest, and it was alleged to hold the Divine autograph of the law written on stone. It also contained the sacred relics of the Hebrews, some of them dating back to the time of Abraham. It is believed, too, that it held the texts which belonged to, or were written by, Moses

THE PYRAMIDS SPEAK

According to legend the box or chest was made of shittim or acacia wood and was without a lid. Later, a crown of gold was added and placed on the rim, with a separate lid made of pure gold. This was called the Mercy-seat. In the Holy Scriptures, Moses says that the Ark of the Covenant was $2\frac{1}{2}$ cubits long, $1\frac{1}{2}$ cubits broad and $1\frac{1}{2}$ cubits high. Sir Isaac Newton's translation indicates that the Ark was $62\frac{1}{2}$ inches x $37\frac{1}{2}$ inches X $37\frac{1}{2}$ inches.

The chest was built 3,300 years ago according to the inspirational commands received by Moses after he left Egypt, and it was the Ark which overthrew the idol gods of the Philistines, and was a source of safety to Israel when used with God's permission.

The Bible does not say what became of the chest. The Eastern Churches say it is in their possession. The Abyssinians claim they have it in their country. Some believe that the Ark was hidden by Jeremiah in Mount Nebo to keep it out of the hands of Nebuchadnezzar when he destroyed Jerusalem. Others feel that the sacred Ark was brought to Tara in Ireland by Jeremiah, and that it is still there in a Masonic preservation.

In Samuel 4 it is stated that the Philistines captured the Ark at Aphek. Scholars now feel that the chest they took was a false ark, and that the real one was whisked away by King David, who placed it in one of the Egyptian pyramids for safekeeping.

What no one knows is which pyramid was selected by David. There are 82 known pyramids. Not all have been thoroughly searched. History also tells us, oddly enough, that the Ark of the Covenant has the same measurements as the open tomb in the King's Chamber of the Great Pyramid.

One thing all scholars agree on is that if the Ark is ever found it will shed light on more mysteries than were illuminated by the Dead Sea Scrolls. It may also tell us the Great Pyramid's connection with the Old Testament, the true origin of the one-God theory of religion, and the source of many Biblical prophecies.

ARE WE IN THE LAST JUDGMENT?

According to the builder-prophets of the Great Pyramid, the Age of Adam will end on September 19, 2001. The book of Revelation says that the children of Adam will be judged, the chosen recognized and the New Jerusalem will be built. Both prophecies indicate a last judgment. If such a cataclysm does come, we don't know who will be left alive to be judged and recognized. There are scholars who feel that in the Book of Revelation, chapter 6, verses 12-17, the prophecies have already taken place. This section reads:

When he opened the sixth seal, I looked, and behold, there was a great earthquake, and the sun turned black as sackcloth, the full moon turned the color of blood, and the stars of the sky fell to the earth as the fig tree sheds its winter fruit when shaken by a mighty wind; the sky vanished like a scroll that is rolled up, and every mountain and island was moved out of its place. Then the kings of the earth and the great men and the generals and the rich and the strong and everyone, slave and free, hid in the caves and among the rocks of the mountains, calling to the mountains and rocks, "Fall on us, and hide us from the face of him, who is seated on the throne, and from the wrath of the lamb. For the great day of their wrath has come, and who can stand before it?"

In 1755 many people thought the prophecy had come true, because in that year there was an earthquake of stupendous proportions. It covered at least eleven million square kilometers and was even felt at sea. Europe, Africa and America were affected. A large part of Algiers was destroyed. In Fez and Mequinez, the dead remained buried in the ruins. The earthquake spread north to Norway, Sweden, Germany, Holland, Great Britain and Ireland. Ninety thousand perished in Lisbon.

The highest mountains in Portugal were shaken. They split open. Many of them broke apart. Flames burst out and great clouds of smoke billowed down over the valleys. Port cities were inundated. In less than six minutes on that November 1st day in 1755, thousands upon thousands of people died. Sailors on ships at sea took such an impact that they were hurled three feet off the decks. If anything qualified as a sign from the sixth seal of the Apocalypse, this was it.

Yet, the earth stopped trembling and life went on. Another prophecy was fulfilled on May 19, 1780, when "the sun turned black as sackcloth." It happened in the United States and all of the New England states were affected. The phenomenon began at ten o'clock in the morning and lasted into the following night. The people were filled with fear. It was so dark that common print could not be read. Candles had to be lighted to complete daily chores, to see clocks, and to walk in the streets. The black sky spread from Maine to Albany, New York. The cause of the blackening of the sun has never been explained.

Perhaps those two incidents were the prophecies outlined in Revelations, chapter six, verses 12-17. Nowhere in that section does it say that the world will come to an end. The prophecy of the Great Pyramid is more specific, giving the actual date of September 17, 2001 as the day the world comes to an end. But how? Here, the Great Pyramid is vague.

THE PYRAMIDS SPEAK

THE LAST DAYS

According to the Great Pyramid, the beginning of the end will be seen in 1987. Then there will be five years of mass confusion, chaos and madness. These words are generalizations We do know that the word cataclysm is used, and that almost 70 percent of the population will be destroyed. The prophecy of the Great Pyramid becomes more specific when it tells us that there will be a gradual normalization of life, with a new climate, a new philosophy, and a new Messiah, who will have been born before the cataclysm. _The new era will begin when the trumpet sounds for the Jewish festival of Yom Kippur, but, says the Great Pyramid, there will be no Jewish nation or congregation on the face of the earth.

A CLUE AS TO HOW THE WORLD WILL END

Not long ago Columbia University scientists discovered a gigantic flaw exists on the ocean floor. The flaw is at least 144,000 miles long, 64 miles wide and has an average depth of four miles. This enormous crack in the earth, due to recent shifts in the crust, runs from the South Pole to the tip of South America, then splits. One branch goes from Chile to Alaska; another from the Philippines to New Zealand. One other branch runs from Japan to the Hawaiian Islands. On the Atlantic side there is a continuation of the flaw which travels from Norway to Portugal and then to Africa, disappearing finally in the Portuguese Guinea Islands. Almost every part of the earth is touched by this flaw.

Scientists blame most of the earthquakes and tremors that are felt around the world on this flaw. What's more, the frequency of these upheavals is increasing. There is also an increase in volcanic eruptions: witness Mount Etna and Mount St. Helens. Actually, erupting volcanoes are safety valves which permit steam from the earth's core to escape. But they can also cause tidal waves. And if the flaws at the oceans' bottoms allow water to reach the molten center, the steam produced will be far greater than anything escaping from a volcano. In fact, the circled flaw in the Pacific Ocean, if sliced deep enough into the earth, could force an explosion that would tear a great portion of the ocean away from the globe.

If too many volcanoes exploded, the earth would be darkened by the huge quantities of dust in the air. The world's temperature would drop. Tidal waves would loosen icebergs which would float toward the Equator, adding to the frigid weather conditions. Freezing rains would swell rivers and lakes. The sea would rise, destroying port cities and even some inland communities.

Is this what the Great Pyramid tells us? We don't know. But from this vantage point it would appear to be the logical transition. It is also more realistic to believe that the world won't end in complete annihilation, with no living thing left, but that there will be enormous changes, as the Great Pyramid suggests.

THE PYRAMIDS SPEAK

PSYCHIC EXPERIENCE IN THE GREAT PYRAMID

In his book, *"A Search in Secret Egypt,"* Dr. Paul Brunton describes how it felt to spend a night alone in the King's Chamber of the Great Pyramid. Dr. Brunton said that the atmosphere and temperature of this chamber have a deathlike cold which cuts to the marrow of the bone. He added that he struck the great coffer, a gigantic monument of stone, to confirm what he had heard about it.

The story was true. The unusual sound produced is impossible to duplicate on any known musical instrument.

Dr. Brunton had some training in Egyptian religion and was well versed in parapsychology. For three days before entering the King's Chamber he touched no food so that he would be receptive to whatever forces were present.

He then sat with his back to the great coffer and turned off his flashlight. He was now aware of a psychic atmosphere. He felt a negative presence. Being human, he felt an almost uncontrollable desire to cut and run. Instead, he forced himself to sit still.

And that was when he became aware of entities that were grossly deformed. They appeared to be testing his sanity. Fear mounted within him, but he fought for self-control. The only thing he was sure of at this point was that he would never again spend a night alone in the King's Chamber of the Great Pyramid.

Quite suddenly, however, the negative forces dissipated. The atmosphere was more friendly now, more alive. He saw two figures who looked like high priests. They spoke, but the words appeared to come into Dr. Brunton's head rather than his ears. One priest asked him why had he come and if the world of mortals wasn't enough for him.

Brunton said, "No, that cannot be."

The other priest warned: "The way of dream will draw thee far from the fold of reason. Some have gone upon it—and come back mad. Turn now, whilst there is yet time and follow the path appointed for mortal feet."

Dr. Brunton insisted on staying. One priest vanished.

The other told the visitor to lie down on the coffer, just as the initiates did in ancient times. Brunton obeyed. He suddenly felt a strange force come over him and that was followed by an out-of-body experience. He was in another dimension. There was little stress. He saw the silver cord linking him to his physical body. He had a feeling of complete freedom.

Brunton then found himself with the other priest, who told him: "Know, my son, that in this ancient fane lies the lost record of the early races of man and the Cov-

THE PYRAMIDS SPEAK

enant which they made with the Creator through the first of His great prophets. Know, too, that chosen men were brought here of old to be shown this Covenant that they might return to their fellows and keep the great secret alive. Take back with thee the warning that when men forsake their Creator and look on their fellows with hate, as with the princes of Atlantis in whose time this pyramid was built, they are destroyed by the weight of their own iniquity, even as the people of Atlantis were destroyed."

When the priest went silent, Brunton found himself back in his body. He felt cumbersome with it. He put on his jacket and made his way to the outside. His watch said midnight. He wasn't sure whether he had had a psychic experience, or if his subconscious played tricks on him.

PYRAMID POWER

In 1949 Karl Drbal, a radio engineer in Prague, Czechoslovakia, filed a patent with the Patent Examination Commission. His invention was a simple cardboard model of the Great Pyramid of Cheops. His premise was that a razor blade, placed in the pyramid's cavity, would have its steel edge sharpened after a period of 24 hours.

It took the Commission ten years to grant Drbal the patent He made it clear that the cardboard pyramid is not a sharpener, but a regenerator. The inventor kept a record of the blades he used for 25 years. From March 3, 1949 to July 6, 1954 he used 18 blades of different brands and was able to achieve an average of 105 shaves per blade. From a single blade he was able to get as many as 200, 170, 165, 111 and 100 shaves. In the 25-year period he used 68 blades.

Drbal said that over the years he has received thousands of letters from pyramid users in the Soviet Union and has yet to receive a letter of complaint. He feels that the blade edge inside the pyramid becomes a living entity in contact with the environmental field. Again and again he took a dull blade, one which gave him a poor shave, and placed it in his pyramid for 24 hours. His next shave with the same blade was perfect!

PYRAMIDS CAN MUMMIFY

Karl Drbal heard about a man named Antoine Bovis who experimented with mummification inside a model pyramid. Bovis tried it after he learned that mummified animals were found in the Great Pyramid of Cheops. It worked! Bovis mummified dead organic matter, meat, eggs, and small dead animals.

Karl Drbal tried it and was able to mummify beef, calf, lamb, eggs, flowers, dead frogs, snakes and lizards. To explain the theory would take volumes. Suffice it to say that the pyramid holds mystical powers that have yet to be fully explained.

THE PYRAMIDS SPEAK

DOES THE PYRAMID SHAPE AROUSE DORMANT GODS?

The basic contention of the "Papyrus of Ani" (an ancient Egyptian text) is that the god who sleeps in the soul of each person is awakened by the energy of the pyramid. Today's mystics say that a homemade pyramid used as a meditation area can stimulate psychic powers. The claim of many is that with the help of the pyramid they are able to reach an altered state of consciousness much quicker. Some say that answers to questions come to them, or that they see visions. And if nothing else, the mystics feel a sense of being at peace with themselves inside a pyramid.

PYRAMID EXPERIMENTS

A psychic research organization in California, called E.S.P. Laboratory, conducted experiments using the pyramid as an incubator for thought-forms. Al Manning, the director of the Los Angeles-based laboratory, said that the pyramid's shape acts as a geometric amplifier. This amplification increases the power of prayer. It will also strengthen the faith of a religious person.

Admittedly, those who have had success with the pyramid shape have had a good deal of occult training. Experimenters used a small cardboard pyramid with triangular sheets of paper in four colors: blue, for healing; green for love; orange for mental clarity; yellow for intuition.

A statement or a goal is written on one of the sheets. If the experimenter, for instance, wanted an answer to a love problem, he would write his request on the green sheet. What is written must be plainly worded. If the request is vague, the experimenter must wait until he has his thought clear in his mind.

The organization provided the experimenters with a chant to be verbalized while the sheet of paper is held between the palms. The chant is spoken twice. After that is done, the apex is folded down and the bottom folded up, so that the sheet ends up folded in thirds. The folded paper is placed on the bottom of the pyramid (base). The pyramid must be aligned in a north-south direction. The palms are placed above the paper and the chant is spoken again. With the pyramid placed over the paper, the incubation period has begun.

The gestation period takes from three to nine days. Once a day there is chanting on the north side of the pyramid. The thought-form is fed into it. It's anybody's guess as to when the right time has arrived to remove the paper from the pyramid, but when it is, it's set on fire. The ashes are dropped into a fireproof receptacle. The burning is done so that the thought-form can be released, and it must be complete, with not a shred of the paper remaining. Fire is considered the most powerful of the four holy elements; with that accomplished the experimenter waits for the fulfillment of his request.

THE PYRAMIDS SPEAK

According to E.S.P. Laboratory, the success rate is phenomenal. People have had their requests satisfied in the form of new jobs, success in business ventures, and health and wealth.

AMAZING RESULTS WITH LIFE-SIZE PYRAMID MODELS

The organization experimented with models six to eight feet high. The experimenters discovered that these pyramid shapes had several energy centers called chakras, which are similar to the energy centers in the human body. More than 80 percent of those who entered these homemade pyramids said that they were able to pinpoint the centers inside the structures

Another large percentage said that they were aware of a warm and soothing feeling once they were inside. Some of the experimenters stated that when they raised their arms toward the pyramid's apex, they felt a pricking sensation, as if small needles were stuck into their hands and arms.

Not all of the areas in the pyramids were beneficial. It was reported that individuals who stood or sat in a particular area suffered headaches after only a short time. In one experiment, three men entered a pyramid and stood talking for a few minutes. When they stepped outside, two of the men experienced vertigo. The third went home and canceled a cocktail party because he was too sleepy to attend it. He fell asleep around 6:30 P.M. When he woke up he felt well-rested and extremely healthy. It was also claimed that pyramids were used to relieve migraine-type headaches.

HEALING POWERS OF THE PYRAMID

The feeling among pyramid advocates is that the structure focuses and intensifies energies that are not really identifiable. Because of this, healing is possible. Another theory is that the atmosphere inside a pyramid stimulates an acceleration of enzyme action. This may account for the effects of mummification, and even the intensity of meditation which is achieved inside a pyramid. Some doctors think that the pyramid might be useful in the treatment of intractable edema and as an aid to organ regeneration. It has been suggested that hospitals of the future may have pyramid-shaped containers for the storing of vital organs.

An experimenter in the Midwest thinks a pyramid might alleviate arthritis or rheumatism. She said the sufferer should place the aching area under the apex of the pyramid to get the full charge of energy.

THE PYRAMID AS A MEDITATION AID

Many pyramid owners use them for meditational purposes. They experience calmness and even extreme euphoria during their sessions. The body relaxes totally. All stress and worry vanish. In most cases they feel a charge of psychic energy. The memory is increased, often to a degree that they can recall their past incarnations. Some meditators see colors, forms, symbols, hear music. Others experience precognition, space travel, telepathic communications and see the answers to their prayers.

PROOF OF A PYRAMID ENERGY FORCE

The energies inside and outside a pyramid, no matter what its size, are measurable. The helical vortex of energy which emanates from the apex is especially powerful. By using dowsing rods, with pyramids made of cardboard only four inches high, dowsers have demonstrated that the energy vortex above the apex can reach a height of almost eight feet. The diameter can be as wide as almost six feet.

In a controlled experiment to prove the existence of a vortex of energy, one miniature pyramid was placed under one of three identical cardboard boxes. A dowser who did not know which box held the pyramid tested each with his rod. The rod reacted only over the box containing the pyramid.

PYRAMID USES

People who have bought or made their own pyramids report various uses. They are being used as razor blade containers or thought-form incubators. Some owners say they store their lottery tickets inside pyramids. It's farfetched to assume that pyramids have the power to produce winning tickets, but allegedly quite a few people have won after storing their lottery tickets in pyramids. And people who are sick or in pain claim that after keeping a pyramid under their chair or bed they saw their pain go away or at least become alleviated.

The late movie actress Gloria Swanson told Time magazine (October 8, 1973) that a pyramid under her bed made every cell in her body tingle. Hollywood actor James Coburn reported in the January 13, 1974 issue of the National Enquirer: "I firmly believe in pyramid power. I crawl inside my pyramid tent, sit in a yoga position, and does it work! It gives off a definite feeling and sensation. It creates an atmosphere that makes it easier to meditate. It closes out all interference. I meditate there every day, between fifteen minutes to an hour."

Some pyramid owners said that they tried sleeping in them but could not do so for more than three nights in a row because they were so energized that they could not cope with the dynamic effects that swept over them.

PYRAMID HATS

Ancient Egyptian priests wore pyramid-shaped hats when they tried to contact their sun god, Ra. Karl Drbal, the man who invented the idea of sharpening razor blades inside pyramids, also conducted experiments with pyramid hats. He was spurred into this direction by noting that witches and sorcerers were also depicted in conical-shaped hats. Some wearers said that pyramid hats were great for relieving headaches. One researcher said that the reason such hats work is that the pyramid acts like a cosmic antenna tuning into sources of energy of vast intensity and then focusing them into its center.

MAGICAL STONES OR AMULETS.

By Wallis Budge

"AMULET" is a name given to a class of objects and ornaments, and articles of dress and wearing apparel, made of various substances which were employed by the Egyptians, and later by other nations, to protect the human body, either living or dead, from baleful influences, and from the attacks of visible and invisible foes. The word "amulet" is derived from an Arabic root meaning "to bear, to carry," hence "amulet" is "something which is carried or worn," and the name is applied broadly to any kind of talisman or ornament to which supernatural powers are ascribed. It is not clear whether the amulet was intended first of all to protect the living or the dead body, but it seems that it was originally worn to guard its owner from savage animals and from serpents. As time went on the development of religious ideas and beliefs progressed, and as a result new amulets representing new views were invented; and the objects which were able to protect the living were made, by an easy transition in the minds of those who wore them, to protect the dead. Moreover, as the preservation of the corruptible body, with the number of its members complete and intact, was of the most vital importance for the life of the spiritual and incorruptible body which was believed to spring therefrom, under the influence of the new beliefs the dead body became a veritable storehouse of amulets. Each member was placed under the specific protection of some amulet, and a number of objects which were believed to protect the body generally from serpents, worms, mildew, decay and putrefaction were laid with a lavish hand in, and upon, and about it, and between the bandages with which it was swathed. When men in Egypt began to lay amulets on their dead cannot be said, and it is equally impossible to say when the belief in the efficacy of such and such an amulet sprang into being; it seems clear, however, that certain amulets represent beliefs and superstitions so old that even the Egyptians were, at times, doubtful about their origin and meaning.

Amulets are of two kinds: (1) those which are inscribed with magical formula, and (2) those which are not. In the earliest times formula or prayers were recited over the amulets that were worn by the living or placed on the dead by priests or men set apart to perform religious services by the community; but it was not in the power of every man to employ them, and at a comparatively early date words of magical power and prayers were cut upon the amulets, which thus became possessed of a twofold power, that is to say, the power which was thought to be inherent in the substance of which the amulet was made, and that which lay in the words inscribed upon it. The earliest name for the formula found upon amulets is *hekau*, and it was so necessary for the deceased to be provided with these hekau, or "words of power," that in the XVIth Century B.C., and probably more than a thousand years earlier, a special section 1 was inserted in the Book of the Dead with the object of causing them to come to him from whatever place they were in, "swifter than greyhounds and quicker than light." The earliest Egyptian amulets known are pieces of green schist, of various shapes, animal and otherwise, which were laid upon the breast of the deceased; these are found in large numbers in the prehistoric or predynastic graves at several places in Egypt. It is most unlikely that they were made by the aboriginal inhabitants of Egypt, for, notwithstanding the various conjectures which have been made as to their object and use, it is pretty certain that, as M. J. de Morgan said, 2 they "belong to the cult." According to this writer their use was exceedingly widespread until the end of the neolithic period, but with the advent of the people whom we call Egyptians they become very rare. In the subsequent period the animal forms disappear, and their place is taken by plaques of schist, rectangular in shape, upon which are inscribed, in rough outline, figures of animals, etc. The theory that these objects were intended as whetstones, or as slabs upon which to rub down paint, will not hold, for the reasons which M. J. de Morgan has given. Moreover, in the green stone scarab which was laid upon the breast of the deceased in dynastic times, we probably have a survival of the green schist amulet of predynastic times in Egypt, both as regards the object with which it was made and the material. But the custom of writing hekau, or words of power, upon papyrus is almost as old as that of writing them upon stone, and we see from the inscription on the walls of the corridors and chambers of the pyramid of Unas, king of Egypt about B.C. 3300, that a "book with words of magical power" was buried with him. 1 Elsewhere 2 we are told that the book which Teta, king of Egypt about B.C. 3266, had with him "hath effect upon the heart of the gods"; and there is no doubt that the object of every religious text ever written on tomb, stele, amulet, coffin, papyrus, etc., was to bring the gods under the power of the deceased, so that he might be able to compel them to do his will.

THE PYRAMIDS SPEAK

1. THE AMULET OF THE HEART

The heart was not only the seat of the power of life, but also the source of both good and evil thoughts; and it sometimes typified the conscience. It was guarded after death with special care, and was mummified separately, and then, with the lungs, was preserved in a jar which was placed under the protection of the god Tuamutef. Its preservation was considered to be of such importance that a text 1 was introduced into the Book of the Dead at an early period, with the view of providing the deceased with a heart in the place of that which had been removed in the process of mummification. The text reads:—

"May my heart be with me in the House of Hearts! May my breast 2 be with me in the House of Hearts! May my heart be with me, and may it rest there, or I shall not eat of the cakes of Osiris on the eastern side of the Lake of Flowers, neither shall I have a boat wherein to go down the Nile, nor another wherein to go up, nor shall I be able to sail down the Nile with thee. May my mouth [be given] to me that I may speak therewith, and my two legs to walk therewith, and my two hands and arms to overthrow my foe. May the doors of heaven be opened unto me; may Seb, the prince of the gods, open wide his two jaws unto me; may he open my two eyes which are blindfolded; may he cause me to stretch apart my two legs which are bound together; and may Anpu (Anubis) make my thighs to be firm so that I may stand upon them. May the goddess Sekhet make me to rise so that I may ascend into heaven, and may that which I command in the House of the Ka of Ptah be done. I shall understand with my heart, I shall gain the mastery over my heart, I shall gain the mastery over my two hands, I shall gain the mastery over my legs, I shall have the power to do whatsoever my *ka* (*i.e.*, double) pleaseth. My soul shall not be fettered to my body at the gates of the underworld, but I shall enter in and come forth in peace."

When the deceased had uttered these words, it was believed that he would at once obtain the powers which he wished to possess in the next world; and when he had gained the mastery over his heart, the heart, the double, and the soul had the power to go where they wished and to do what they pleased. The mention of the god Ptah and of his consort Sekhet indicates that the Chapter was the work of the priests of Memphis, and that the ideas embodied in it are of great antiquity. According to the Papyrus of Nekhtu-Amen, the amulet of the heart, which is referred to in the above Chapter, was to be made of lapis-lazuli, and there is no doubt that this stone was believed to possess certain qualities which were beneficial to those who wore it. It will also be remembered that, according to one tradition, [1] the text of the LXIVth Chapter of the Book of the Dead was found written in letters of lapis-lazuli in the reign of Hesep-ti, king of Egypt about B.C. 4300, and the way in which the fact is mentioned in the Rubric to the Chapter proves that special importance was attached to it.

Nefer-uben-f, a priest, guarding his heart against the destroyer of hearts.(From Naville, Todtenbuch, vol. I. plate 39.)

But although a heart might be given to a man by means of the above Chapter, it was necessary for the deceased to take the greatest care that it was not carried off from him by a monster, who was part man and part beast, and who went about seeking for hearts to carry away. To prevent such a calamity no less than seven Chapters of the Book of the Dead (Nos. XXVII., XXVIII., XXIX., XXIXA, XXX., XXXA, and XXXB) were written. The XXVIIth Chapter was connected with a heart amulet made of a white, semitransparent stone, and reads:—

"Hail, ye who carry away hearts! Hail, ye who steal hearts, and who make the heart of a man to go through its transformations according to its deeds, let not what he hath done harm him before you! Homage to you, O ye lords of eternity, ye possessors of ever lastingness, take ye not this heart of Osiris [1] into your grasp, and cause ye not words of evil to spring up against it; for it is the heart of Osiris, and it belongeth unto him of many names, 2 the mighty one whose words are his limbs, and who sendeth forth his heart to dwell in his body. The heart of Osiris is triumphant, and it is made new before the gods: he hath gained power over it, and he hath not been judged according to what he hath done. He hath gotten power over his own members. His heart obeyeth him, he is the lord thereof, it is in his body, and it shall never fall away therefrom. I, Osiris, victorious in peace, and triumphant in the beautiful Amenta and on the mountain of eternity, bid thee [O heart] to be obedient unto me in the underworld."

Another Chapter (XXIXB) was connected with a heart amulet made of carnelian, of which so many examples may be found in large museums; the text reads: "I am the Bennu, 1 the soul of Râ, and the guide of the gods who are in the underworld. Their divine souls came forth upon earth to do the will of their doubles, let therefore the soul of the Osiris come forth to do the will of his double." The Bennu was also the soul of Osiris, and thus the amulet brought with it the protection of both Osiris and Râ.

But of all the Chapters which related to the heart, the most popular among the Egyptians was that which is commonly known as XXXB, and its importance from a religious point of view cannot be overstated. The antiquity of the Chapter is undoubted, for according to the Papyrus of Nu, 2 a document of the early part of the XVIIIth dynasty, it dates from the time of Hesep-ti, king of Egypt about B.C. 4300, and it seems that it formed a pendant or supplement to the LXIVth Chapter, which professed to give the substance of all the "Chapters of Coming Forth by Day" in a single Chapter. In the rubric to the longer version of the Chapter, given in the same papyrus, 3 Chapter XXXB is connected with Herutâtâf, the son of Khufu (Cheops), a man famed for wisdom, and it is there ordered that the words of it be recited over a hard, green stone scarab, which shall be laid in the breast of the deceased where the heart would ordinarily be; this amulet would then perform for him the "opening of the mouth," 1 for the words of the Chapter would be indeed "words of power." From reciting the words of the Chapter over a scarab to engraving them upon it was but a step, and this step was taken as early as the IVth dynasty. The text is as follows:—

"My heart, my mother; my heart, my mother! My heart whereby I came into being! May naught stand up to oppose me at [my] judgment; may there be no opposition to me in the presence of the sovereign princes; may there be no parting of thee from me in the presence of him that keepeth the Balance! Thou art my double (*ka*), the dweller in my body, the god Khnemu who knitteth and strengtheneth my limbs. Mayest thou come forth into the place of happiness whither we go. May the *Shenit*, who form the conditions of the lives of men, not make my name to stink. Let it be satisfactory unto us, and let the listening be satisfactory unto us, and let there be joy of heart unto us at the weighing of words. Let not that which is false be uttered against me before the great god, the lord of Amentet. Verily how great shalt thou be when thou risest in triumph."

It was this Chapter which the deceased recited when he was in the Judgment Hall of Osiris, whilst his heart was being weighed in the Balance against the feather symbolic of right and truth. From certain papyri it seems as if the above words should, properly be said by the deceased when he is being weighed against his own heart, a conception which is quite different from that of the judgment of the heart before the gods.

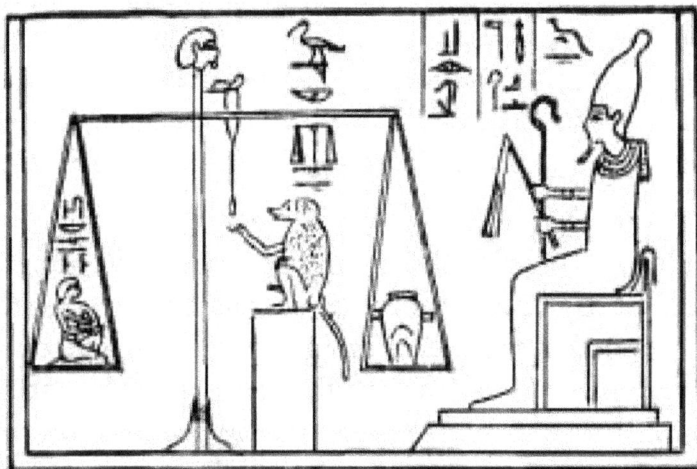

The scribe Nebsent being weighed in a balance against his heart in the presence of Osiris. (From the Papyrus of Nebsent, sheet 4.)

2. THE AMULET OF THE SCARAB

From what has been said above it will be seen that the amulet of the heart, which was connected with the most important and most popular of the Chapters for protecting the heart, was directed to be made in the form of the scarab at a very early date. We can trace the ideas which the Egyptians held about this insect as far back as the time of the building of the Pyramids, [1] and there is no doubt that they represented beliefs which even at that early period were very old. The Egyptian seems to have reasoned thus: since the physical heart is taken from the body before mummification, and the body has need of another to act as the source of life and movement in its new life, another must be put in its place. But a stone heart, whether made of lapis-lazuli or carnelian, is only a stone heart after all, and even though by means of prayers properly recited it prevents the physical heart from being carried off by "those who plunder hearts," it possesses nothing of itself which can be turned to account in giving new life and being to the body on which it lies. But the scarab or beetle itself possesses remarkable powers, and if a figure of the scarab be made, and the proper words of power be written upon it, not only protection of the dead physical heart, but also new life and existence will be given to him to whose body it is attached. Moreover, the scarab was the type and symbol of the god Khepera, the invisible power of creation which propelled the sun across the sky. The particular beetle chosen by the Egyptians to copy for amulets belongs to the family of dung-feeding Lamellicorns which live in tropical countries. The species are generally of a black hue, but amongst them are to be found some adorned with the richest metallic colors. A remarkable peculiarity exists in the structure and situation of the hind legs, which are placed so near the extremity of the body, and so far from each other, as to give the insect a most extraordinary appearance when walking. This peculiar formation is, nevertheless, particularly serviceable to its possessors in rolling the balls of excrementitious matter in which they enclose their eggs. These balls are at first irregular and soft, but, by degrees, and during the process of rolling along, become rounded and harder; they are propelled by means of the hind legs. Sometimes these balls are an inch and a half or two inches in diameter, and in rolling them along the beetles stand almost upon their heads, with the heads turned from the balls. These maneuvers have for their object the burying of the balls in holes, which the insects have previously dug for their reception; and it is upon the dung thus deposited that the larva, when hatched, feed. It does not appear that these beetles have the ability to distinguish their own balls, as they will seize upon those belonging to another, in the case of their having lost their own; indeed, it is said that several of them occasionally assist in rolling the same ball. The males as well as the females assist in rolling the pellets. They fly during the hottest part of the day. 1

Among the ancients several curious views were held about the scarab, whether of the type *scarabæus sacer* or the *ateuchus Ægyptiorium*, 2 and Ælian, Porphyry, and Horapollo declared that no female scarab existed. The last named writer stated that the scarab denoted "only begotten," because it was a creature self-produced, being unconceived by a female. He goes on to say that, having made a ball of dung, the beetle rolls it from east to west, and having dug a hole, he buries it in it for eight and twenty days; on the twenty-ninth day he opens the ball, and throws it into the water, and from it the scarabæi come forth. The fact that the scarab flies during the hottest part of the day made the insect to be identified with the sun, and the ball of eggs to be compared to the sun itself. The unseen power of God, made manifest under the form of the god Khepera, caused the sun to roll across the sky, and the act of rolling gave to the scarab its name *kheper*, *i.e.*, "he who rolls." The sun contained the germs of all life, and as the insect's ball contained the germs of the young scarabs it was identified also with the sun as a creature which produced life in a special way. Now, the god Khepera also represented inert but living matter, which was about to begin a course of existence, and at a very early period he was considered to be a god of the resurrection; and since the scarab was identified with him that insect became at once the symbol of the god and the type of the resurrection. But the dead human body, from one aspect, contained the germ of life, that is to say, the germ of the spiritual body, which was called into being by means of the prayers that were recited and the ceremonies that were performed on the day of the funeral; from this point of view the insect's egg ball and the dead body were identical. Now, as the insect had given potential life to its eggs in the ball, so, it was thought, would a model of the scarab, itself the symbol of the god Khepera, also give potential life to the dead body upon which it was placed, always provided that the proper "words of power" were first said over it or written upon it. The idea of "life" appears to have attached itself to the scarab from time immemorial in Egypt and the Eastern Sûdân, for to this day the insect is dried, pounded, and mixed with water, and then drunk by women who believe it to be an unfailing specific for the production of large families. In ancient days when a man wished to drive away the effects of every kind of sorcery and incantations he might do so by cutting off the head and wings of a large beetle, which he boiled and laid in oil. The head and wings were then warmed up and steeped in the oil of the *âpnent* serpent, and when they had been once more boiled the man was to drink the mixture. 1

The amulet of the scarab has been found in Egypt in untold thousands, and the varieties are exceedingly numerous. They are made of green basalt, green granite, limestone, green marble, blue paste, blue glass, purple, blue and green glazed porcelain, etc.; and the words of power are usually cut in outline on the base. In rare instances, the scarab has a human face or head, and sometimes the backs are inscribed with figures of the boat of Râ, of the *Bennu* bird, "the soul of Râ," and of the eye of Horus. The green stone scarabs are often set in gold, and have a band of gold across and down the back where the wings join; sometimes the whole back is gilded, and sometimes the base is covered with a plate of gold upon which the words of power have been stamped or engraved. Occasionally the base of the scarab is made in the form of a heart, a fact which proves the closeness of the relationship which existed between the amulets of the heart and scarab. In late times, that is to say about B.C. 1200, large funeral scarabs were set in pylon-shaped pectorals, made of porcelain of various colors, upon which the boat of the Sun was either traced in colors or worked in relief, and the scarab is placed so as to appear to be carried in the boat; on the left stands Isis and on the right Nephthys. 1

THE PYRAMIDS SPEAK

The oldest green stone funeral scarab known to me is in the British Museum (No. 29,224); it was found at Kûrna near Thebes and belongs to the period of the XIth dynasty, about B.C. 2600. The name of the man for whom it was made (he appears to have been an official of the Temple of Amen) was traced on it in light colored paint which was afterwards varnished; there are no "words of power" on this interesting object.

The scribe Ani holding a necklace with pectoral, on which is a figure of the boat of Râ containing a scarab, or beetle, in the presence of Anubis, the god of the dead. (From the Papyrus of Ani, plate 15.)

When once the custom of burying scarabs with the bodies of the dead became recognized, the habit of wearing them as ornaments by the living came into fashion, and as a result scarabs of almost every sort and kind may be found by the thousand in many collections, and it is probable that the number of varieties of them was only limited by the ability of those who manufactured them in ancient days to invent new sorts. The use of the scarab amulet passed into Western Asia and into several countries which lay on the Mediterranean, and those who wore it seem to have attached to it much the same idea as its early inventors, the Egyptians. From a Greek magical papyrus translated by Goodwin 1 we may see that certain solemn ceremonies were performed over a scarab before it was worn, even in the period of the rule of the Greeks and Romans. Thus about the "ring of Horus" and the "ceremony of the beetle" we are told to take a beetle, sculptured as described below, and to place it on a paper table, and under the table there shall be a pure linen cloth; under it put some olive wood, and set on the middle of the table a small censer wherein myrrh and kyphi shall be offered. And have at hand a small vessel of chrysolite into which ointment of lilies, or myrrh, or cinnamon, shall be put, and take the ring and lay it in the ointment, having first made it pure and clean, and offer it up in the censer with kyphi and myrrh; leave the ring for three days, and take it out and put it in a safe place. At the celebration let there lie near at hand some pure loaves, and such fruits as are in season, and having made another sacrifice upon vine sticks, during the sacrifice take the ring out of the ointment, and anoint thyself with the unction from it. Thou shalt anoint thyself early in the morning, and turning towards the east shalt pronounce the words written below. The beetle shall be carved out of a precious emerald; bore it and pass a gold wire through it, and beneath the beetle carve the holy Isis, and having consecrated it as above written, use it. The proper days for the celebration were the 7th, 9th, 10th, 12th, 14th, 16th, 21st, 24th, and 25th, from the beginning of the month; on other days abstain. The spell to be recited began, "I am Thoth," the inventor and founder of medicines and letters; "come to me, thou that art under the earth, rise up to me, thou great spirit."

3. THE AMULET OF THE BUCKLE

This amulet represents the buckle of the girdle of Isis, and is usually made of carnelian, red jasper, red glass, and of other substances of a red color; it is sometimes made of gold, and of substances covered with gold. It is always associated with the CLVIth Chapter of the Book of the Dead, which is frequently inscribed upon it, and which reads:—

"The blood of Isis, and the strength of Isis, and the words of power of Isis shall be mighty to act as powers to protect this great and divine being, and to guard him from him that would do unto him anything that he holdeth in abomination."

But before the buckle was attached to the neck of the deceased, where the rubric ordered it to be placed, it had to be dipped in water in which *ânkham* flowers had been steeped; and when the words of the Chapter of the Buckle given above had been recited over it, the amulet brought to the deceased the protection of the blood of Isis, and of her words of power. It will be remembered that she raised the dead body of Osiris by means of her words of power, and there is a legend to the effect that she smote the Sun-god Râ with severe sickness by the magical power which she possessed. Another object of the buckle was to give the deceased access to every place in the underworld, and to enable him to have "one hand towards heaven, and one hand towards earth."

4. THE AMULET OF THE TET

This amulet probably represents the tree trunk in which the goddess Isis concealed the dead body of her husband, and the four crossbars indicate the four cardinal points; it became a symbol of the highest religious importance to the Egyptians, and the setting up of the Tet at Busiris, which symbolized the reconstituting of the body of Osiris, was one of the most solemn of all the ceremonies performed in connection with the worship of Osiris. The Tet represents neither the mason's table nor a Nilometer, as some have thought, It is always associated with the CLVth Chapter of the Book of the Dead, which reads:—

"Rise up thou, O Osiris! Thou hast thy backbone, O Still-Heart! Thou hast the fastenings of thy neck and back, O Still-Heart! Place thou thyself upon thy base, I put water beneath thee, and I bring unto thee a Tet of gold that thou mayest rejoice therein."

Like the buckle, the Tet had to be dipped in the water in which ânkham flowers had been steeped, and laid upon the neck of the deceased, to whom it gave the power to reconstitute the body and to become a perfect KHU (*i.e.*, spirit) in the underworld. On coffins the right hand of the deceased grasps the buckle, and the left the Tet; both are made of wood, notwithstanding the fact that the rubric to the Chapter of the Te orders the Tet to be made of gold.

The mummy of Ani the scribe, lying on a bier, attended by Isis, Nephthys, Anubis, the four children of Horus, the ushabti figure, his soul, the TET, etc. (From the Papyrus of Ani, plates 33, 34).

5. THE AMULET OF THE PILLOW

This amulet is a model of the pillow which is found placed under the neck of the mummy in the coffin, and its object is to "lift up" and to protect the head of the deceased; it is usually made of hematite, and is inscribed with the text of the CLXVIth Chapter of the Book of the Dead, which reads:—

THE PYRAMIDS SPEAK

"Thou art lifted up, O sick one that liest prostrate. They lift up thy head to the horizon, thou art raised up, and dost triumph by reason of what hath been done for thee. Ptah hath overthrown thine enemies, which was ordered to be done for thee. Thou art Horus, the son of Hathor, . . . who givest back the head after the slaughter. Thy head shall not be carried away from thee after [the slaughter], thy head shall never, never be carried away from thee."

6. THE AMULET OF THE VULTURE

This amulet was intended to cause the power of Isis as the "divine mother" to be a protection for the deceased, and was made of gold in the form of a vulture hovering in the air with outstretched wings and holding in each talon the symbol of "life" and was placed on the neck on the day of the funeral. With this amulet the CLVIIth Chapter of the Book of the Dead was associated, and it was ordered by the rubric to it to be recited over it; this text reads:—

"Isis cometh and hovereth over the city, and she goeth about seeking the secret habitations of Horus as he emergeth from his papyrus swamps, and she raiseth up his shoulder which is in evil case. He is made one of the company in the divine boat, and the sovereignty of the whole world is decreed for him. He hath warred mightily, and he maketh his deeds to be remembered; he hath made the fear of him to exist and awe of him to have its being. His mother the mighty lady, protecteth him, and she hath transferred her power unto him." The first allusion is to the care which Isis shewed for Horus when she was bringing him up in the papyrus swamps, and the second to his combat with Set, whom he vanquished through the might of Isis.

7. THE AMULET OF THE COLLAR OF GOLD

This amulet was intended to give the deceased power to free himself from his swathings; it is ordered by the rubric to the CLVIIIth Chapter of the Book of the Dead to be placed on his neck on the day of the funeral, and to be made of gold. The text of the Chapter reads:—"O my father, my brother, my mother Isis, I am unswathed, and I see. I am one of those who are unswathed and who see the god Seb." This amulet is very rare, and appears to have been the expression of beliefs which grew up in the period of the XXVIth dynasty, about B.C. 550.

8. THE AMULET OF THE PAPYRUS SCEPTRE

This amulet was intended to give the deceased vigor and renewal of youth; it was made of mother-of-emerald, or of light green or blue porcelain, and, when the words of the CLIXth Chapter of the Book of the Dead had been recited over it, it was placed on his neck on the day of the funeral. In the XXVIth dynasty and later it seems as if the amulet represented the power of Isis, who derived it from her father, the husband of Renenet, the goddess of abundant harvests and food. At an earlier period, judging from the text of the CLXth Chapter, the amulet is put by the god Thoth into the hands of the deceased, who says, "It is in sound state, and I am in sound state; it is not injured, and I am not injured; it is not worn away, and I am not worn away."

THE PYRAMIDS SPEAK

9. THE AMULET OF THE SOUL

This amulet was made of gold inlaid with precious stones in the form of a human-headed hawk, and, when the words of the LXXXIXth Chapter of the Book of the Dead had been recited over it, it was directed by the rubric to the Chapter to be placed upon the breast of the deceased. The object of the amulet is apparent from the text in which the deceased is made to say, "Hail, thou god Anniu! Hail, thou god Pehrer, who dwellest in thy hall! Grant thou that my soul may come unto me from wheresoever it may be. If it would tarry, then let my soul be brought unto me from wheresoever it may be. . . . Let me have possession of my soul and of my spirit, and let me be true of voice with them wheresoever they may be. . . . Hail, ye gods, who tow along the boat of the lord of millions of years, who bring it above the underworld, and who make it to travel over Nut, who make souls to enter into their spiritual bodies, . . . grant that the soul of the Osiris 1 "may come forth before the gods, and that it may be true of voice with you in the east of the sky, and follow unto the place where it was yesterday, and enjoy twofold peace in Amentet. May it look upon its natural body, may it rest upon its spiritual body, and may its body neither perish nor suffer corruption for ever!" Thus the amulet of the soul was intended to enable the soul both to unite with the mummified body, and to be with its spirit (*khu*) and spiritual body at will.

10. THE AMULET OF THE LADDER

In tombs of the Ancient and Middle Empires small objects of wood and other substances in the form of ladders have often been found, but the signification of them is not always apparent. From the texts inscribed upon the walls of the corridors and chambers of the pyramids of Unas, Teta, Pepi, and other early kings, it is clear that the primitive Egyptians believed that the floor of heaven, which also formed the sky of this world, was made of an immense plate of iron, rectangular in shape, the four corners of which rested upon four pillars which served to mark the cardinal points. On this plate of iron lived the gods and the blessed dead, and it was the aim of every good Egyptian to go there after death. At certain sacred spots the edge of the plate was so near the tops of the mountains that the deceased might easily clamber on to it and so obtain admission into heaven, but at others the distance between it and the earth was so great that he needed help to reach it. There existed a belief that Osiris himself experienced some difficulty of getting up to the iron plate, and that it was only by means of the ladder which his father Râ provided that he at length ascended into heaven. On one side of the ladder stood Râ, and on the other stood Horus, 1 the son of Isis, and each god assisted Osiris to mount it. Originally the two guardians of the ladder were Horus the Elder and Set, and there are several references in the early texts to the help which they rendered to the deceased, who was, of course, identified with the god Osiris.

But, with a view either of reminding these gods of their supposed duty, or of compelling them to do it, the model of a ladder was often placed on or near the dead body in the tomb, and a special composition was prepared which had the effect of making the ladder become the means of the ascent of the deceased into heaven. Thus in the text written for Pepi 2 the deceased is made to address the ladder in these words: "Homage to thee, O divine Ladder! Homage to thee, O Ladder of Set! Stand thou upright, O divine Ladder! Stand thou upright, O Ladder of Set! Stand thou upright, O Ladder of Horus, whereby Osiris came forth into heaven when he made use of his magical power upon Râ. . . . For Pepi is thy son, and Pepi is Horus, and thou hast given birth unto Pepi even as thou hast given birth unto the god who is the lord of the Ladder (*i.e.*, Horus); and thou shalt give unto Pepi the Ladder of the god (*i.e.*, Horus), thou shalt give unto him the Ladder of the god Set whereby this Pepi shall come forth into heaven when he shall have made use of his magical power upon Râ. O 'thou god of those whose doubles (*kau*) pass onwards, (when the Eye of Horus soareth upon the wing of 'Thoth on the east side of the divine Ladder (or Ladder of God), O men whose bodies [would go] into heaven, Pepi is the Eye of Horus, and when the 'Eye turneth itself to any place where he is, Pepi goeth side by side with the Eye of Horus, and O ye who are the brethren of the gods, rejoice ye that Pepi journeyeth among you. And the brethren of Pepi who axe the gods shall be glad when they meet Pepi, even as Horus is glad when he meeteth his Eye. He hath placed his Eye before his father Seb, and every god and every spirit stretcheth out his hand towards Pepi when he cometh forth into heaven from the Ladder. Pepi hath need neither to 'plough the earth,' nor to 'collect the offering'; and he hath (need neither to go to the Hall which is in Annu (Heliopolis), nor to the Hall of the Morning which is in Annu; for that which he seeth and that which he heareth shall feed him and nourish him when he appeareth in heaven from the Ladder. Pepi riseth like the uraeus on the forehead of Set, and every god and every spirit stretcheth out his hand to Pepi on the Ladder. Pepi hath gathered together his bones, be hath collected his flesh, and he hath gone quickly into heaven by means of the two fingers [1] of the god of the Ladder (*i.e.*, Horus). Elsewhere [2] the gods Khonsu, Sept, etc., are invoked to bring the ladder to Pepi, and the ladder itself is adjured to come with its name, and in another place [3] we read, Homage to thee, O thou Ladder that supportest the golden vase of the Spirits of Pe and the Spirits of Nekhen, stretch out thy hand to this Pepi, and let him take his seat between the two great gods who (care in the place of this Pepi; take him by the hand and lead him towards Sekhet-Hetep (*i.e.*, the Elysian Fields), and let him take his seat among the stars which are in the sky."

In the Theban Recension of the Book of the Dead the importance of the ladder is also seen, for in Chapter CXLIX. [4] the deceased says, "I set up a Ladder among the gods, and I am a divine being among them"; and in Chapter CLIII he says, "The Osiris Nu shall come forth upon your Ladder which Râ hath made for him, and Horus and Set shall grasp him firmly by the hand." Finally, when the custom of placing a model of the ladder in the tomb fell into disuse, the priests provided for the necessity of the dead by painting a ladder on the papyri that were inscribed with the texts from the Book of the Dead and were buried with them. [1]

11. THE AMULET OF THE TWO FINGERS

This amulet is intended to represent the two fingers, index and medius, which the god Horus employed in helping his father Osiris up the ladder [2] into heaven, as has been described above; it is found in the interior of mummies and is usually made of obsidian or hematite.

12. THE AMULET OF THE EYE OF HORUS

The Eye of Horus amulet, or Utchat, is one of the commonest of all, and its use seems to have been universal at all periods. It was made of gold, silver, granite, hematite, carnelian, lapis-lazuli, porcelain, wood, etc., although the rubric of a late Chapter of the Book of the Dead [3] directs that the amulet should be made either of lapis-lazuli or of *mak* stone. The Utchat is of two kinds, one facing to the left and the other to the right, and together they represent the two eyes of Horus, one of which, according to an ancient text, was white and the other black; from another point of view one Utchat represents the Sun and the other the Moon, or Râ and Osiris respectively. But speaking generally, when the Egyptians wore the Utchat as an amulet they intended it to bring to them the blessings of strength, vigor, protection, safety, good health, and the like, and they had in their minds the Eye of Horus, probably the white one, or the Sun. In religious texts the expression *meh Utchat*, i.e., the "filling of the Utchat," is often used, and from many considerations it is clear that we must understand it to refer to the Sun at the summer solstice; thus the amulet seems to have been intended to bring to its wearer strength and health similar to that of the Sun at the season of the year when it is most powerful. In the CLXVIIth Chapter of the Book of the Dead the deceased is made to say, "The god Thoth hath brought the Utchat, and he hath made it to rest after it departed, O Râ. It was grievously afflicted by the storm, but Thoth made it to rest after it departed out of the storm. I am sound, and it is sound; I am sound, and it is sound; and Nebseni, the lord of piety, is sound." To obtain the full benefit of the Utchat amulet for the deceased it was obligatory to make one in lapis-lazuli and to plate it with gold, and then to offer to it offerings at the summer solstice; another had then to be made of jasper and, if after the specified Chapter (CXL.) had been recited over it, it was laid on any part of the body of the deceased, he would become a god and take his place in the boat of Râ. At this solstice twelve altars 1 had to be lighted, four for Râ-Temu, four for the Utchat, and four for the other gods who had been mentioned in the Chapter. An interesting example of the use of the *utchat* occurs in a Greek spell for the discovery of a thief written as late as the IVth century of our era. 2 In it we are told to "take the herb *khelkbei* and *bugloss*, press out the juice and burn the crushed leaves and mix the ashes with the juice. Anoint and write upon a wall Khoô with these materials. And take a common piece of wood, and cut a hammer out of it, and strike with it upon the ear, pronouncing this spell:— 'I adjure thee by the holy names, render up the thief, who has carried away such [and such] a thing Khalkhak, Khalkoum, Khiam, Khar, Khroum, Zbar, Bêri, Zbarkom, Khrê, Kariôb, Pharibou, and by the terrible names {Greek *aeehhhiiiioooooouuuuuuwwwwwww*}'" 3 Following these words we have a picture of the utchat with an arrangement of certain vowels on each side of it thus:

{Greek *wuuiiiihhhhheeeeeeaaaaaaa*}   {Greek *aeehhhiiiihhhhheeeeeeaaaaaaa*}

The spell continues, "Render up the thief who has stolen such [and such] a thing: as long as I strike the ear with this hammer, let the eye of the thief be smitten and inflamed until it betrays him.' Saying these words strike with the hammer." [1]

13. THE AMULET OF "LIFE," (ÂNKH)

The object which is represented by this amulet is unknown, and of all the suggestions which have been made concerning it none is more unlikely than that which would give it a phallic origin. Whatever it may represent, it certainly symbolizes "life"; every god carries it, and it seems, even in the earliest times, to be a conventional representation of some object which in the remotest period had been used as an amulet. In the Papyrus of Ani (2nd edit., plate 2) the Ânkh rises from the Tet, and the arms which project from it support the disk of the sun as here seen. This amulet is made of various substances, and was chiefly employed as a pendant of a necklace.

14. THE AMULET NEFER

This amulet signifies "happiness, good luck," etc., and represents a musical instrument; it was made of carnelian, red stone, red porcelain, and the like, and was a very favorite form for the pendants of necklaces and strings of beads.

15. THE AMULET OF THE SERPENT'S HEAD

This amulet was placed on the dead body to keep it from being bitten by snakes in the underworld or tomb. It is made of red stone, red jasper, red paste, and carnelian. As the goddess Isis is often typified by a serpent, and red is a color peculiar to her, it seems as if the idea underlying the use of this amulet was to vanquish the snakes in the tomb by means of the power of the great snake-goddess Isis. This power had been transferred to it by means of the words of the XXXIVth Chapter of the Book of the Dead, which are often inscribed upon it. The text reads: "O Serpent! I am the flame which shineth upon the Opener of hundreds of thousands of years, and the standard of the god Tenpu," or as others say, "the standard of young plants and flowers. Depart ye from me, for I am the divine Lynx." Some have thought that the snake's head represents the serpent which surmounts the ram's head on the *urhekau* instrument used in performing the ceremony of "Opening the mouth." [1]

The Kher-heb priest touching the statue of the deceased with the urhekau instrument to effect the "opening of the mouth." (From the Papyrus of Ani, plate 15)

16. THE AMULET OF THE MENAT

This amulet was in use in Egypt as early as the VIth dynasty, and it was worn or held or carried with the sistrum by gods, kings, priests, priestesses, etc.; usually it is held in the hand, but it is often worn on the neck. Its object was to bring joy and health to the wearer, and it was believed to possess magical properties; it represented nutrition 2 and strength, and the might of the male and female organs of generation, mystically considered, was supposed to be united therein. The amulet is made in bronze, stone, porcelain, and other substances, and when laid upon the body of the dead brought to it the power of life and reproduction.

17. THE AMULET OF THE SAM

This amulet is probably intended to represent an organ of the human body, and its use is very ancient; it is made of lapis-lazuli and other hard stone substances, and in the late period is often found in the swathings of mummies. Its primary meaning is "union," and refers to animal pleasure.

18. THE AMULET OF THE SHEN

This amulet is intended to represent the sun's orbit, and it became the symbol of an undefined period of time, i.e., eternity; it was laid upon the body of the dead with the view of giving to it life which should endure as long as the sun revolved in its orbit in the heavens. In the picture of the mummy chamber 1 the goddesses Isis and Nephthys are seen kneeling and resting their hands on *shen*. Figures of the *shen* were painted upon stelæ, coffins, etc.; as an amulet it is commonly made of lapis-lazuli or carnelian. The amulet of the cartouche has been supposed to be nothing more than *shen* elongated, but it probably refers to the ordinary meaning of *i.e.*, "name."

19. THE AMULET OF THE STEPS

This amulet seems to have two meanings: to lift up to heaven, and the throne of Osiris. According to one legend, when the god Shu wished to lift up the goddess Nut from the embrace of the god Seb, so that her body, supported by her stretched-out arms and legs, might form the sky, he found that he was not tall enough to do so; in this difficulty he made use of a flight of steps, and having mounted to the top of these he found himself able to perform his work. In the fourth section of the Elysian Fields 1 three such flights of steps are depicted. In the XXIInd Chapter of the Book of the Dead the deceased prays that he "may have a portion with him who is on the top of the steps," *i.e.*, Osiris, and in funeral vignettes this god is seen seated upon the top of a flight of steps and holding his usual symbols of sovereignty and dominion. The amulet of the Steps is usually made of green or blue glazed porcelain.

20. THE AMULET OF THE FROG

This amulet is typical of teeming life and of the resurrection. The frog-headed goddess Heqt, the wife of Khnemu, was associated with the resurrection, and this amulet, when laid upon the body of the dead, was intended to transfer to it her power. The frog is often represented on the upper part of the Greek and Roman terra-cotta lamps which are found in Egypt, and on one of them written in Greek is the legend, "I am the resurrection." 1

The amulets described above are those which are most commonly found in the tombs and on mummies, but a few others are also known, *e.g.*,

THE PYRAMIDS SPEAK

the White crown of the South,

the Red crown of the North,

the horizon, or place where the sun rises,

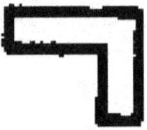

an angle, typifying protection,

the horns, disk, and   plumes,

or the plummet, etc.

Besides these, any ring, or pendant, or ornament, or any object whatsoever, upon which was inscribed the name of a god or his emblem, or picture, became an amulet with protective powers; and it seems that these powers remained active as long as the substance lasted and as long as the name, or emblem, or picture, was not erased from it. The use of amulets was common in Egypt from the earliest times to the Roman Period, and when the Egyptians embraced Christianity, they, in common with the Gnostics and semi-Christian sects, imported into their new faith many of the views and beliefs which their so-called heathen ancestors had held, and with them the use of the names of ancient Egyptian gods, and goddesses, and demons, and formulæ, which they employed in much the same way as they were employed in the days of old.

Footnotes

27:1 *I.e.*, Chapter XXIV., which is entitled, "The Chapter of bringing words of power unto Osiris in the underworld."

27:2 *Ethnographie Prehistorique*, p. 144.

28:1 *Unas*, ed. Maspero, line 584.

28:2 *Teta*, ed. Maspero, line 351.

29:1 Chapter XXVI., entitled, "The Chapter of giving a heart to the deceased."

29:2 Literally, "pericardium."

31:1 See Chapters of Coming Forth by Day (translation, p. 119).

32:1 *I.e.*, the deceased who was identified with Osiris, the god and judge of the dead.

32:2 *I.e.*, Thoth.

33:1 The Bennu bird is usually identified with the phoenix.

33:2 Brit. Mus., No. 10,477, sheet 13.

33:3 See sheet 21.

34:1 See Chapter VI. (Magical Ceremonies).

35:1 King Teta is said to "live like the scarab" (*Teta*, line 89); and in it is said, "Pepi is the son of the Scarab which is born in Hetepet under the hair of the northern Iusâas" (*Pepi*, line 422).

37:1 See J. O. Westwood, *Introduction to the Modern Classification of Insects*, London, 1839, vol. i. p. 204 ff.

37:2 See my *Mummy*, p. 233.

39:1 See Joachim, *Das älteste Buch über Heilkunde*, Berlin, 1800, p. 160.

41:1 have given a summary of the chief varieties of the funeral scarab in my *Papyrus of Ani*, London, 1895, p. 262.

42:1 *Fragment of a Græco-Egyptian Work upon Magic* (Publications of the Cambridge Antiquarian Society, 1852).

50:1 *I.e.*, the deceased, who is identified with the god Osiris.

52:1 *Unas*, line 579.

52:2 Line 192 f.

54:1 Compare, "Give thou to Pepi these two fingers which thou hast given to Nefert, the daughter of the great god, as messengers from heaven to earth" (*Pepi*, line 422).

54:2 Pepi, line 200.

54:3 Pepi, line 471.

54:4 See my *Chapters of Coming Forth by Day*, translation, p. 270.

55:1 See the Papyrus of Ani, 2nd edition, pl. 22.

55:2 See Pepi, line 196.

55:3 *I.e.*, CXL.

57:1 One for each month of the year.

57:2 Kenyon, *Catalogue of Greek Papyri*, p. 61.

57:3 The seven vowels were supposed in the Gnostic system to contain all the names of God, and were, therefore, most powerful when used as a spell.

58:1 See Goodwin, Fragment of a Græco-Egyptian work upon Magic, p. 7.

60:1 See the description of this ceremony in Chapter VI.

60:2 *Menat* is connected with the root from which the word for "nurse" (*menât*) is derived; see the article by Lefébure, "Le Menat et le Nom de l'Eunuque" in *Proc. Soc. Bibl. Arch.*, 1891, p. 333 f.

61:1 See *Papyrus of Ani*, 2nd edit, plates 33, 31.

62:1 See *Papyrus of Ani*, 2nd edit., plate 35.

63:1 See Lanzone, *Dizionario*, p. 853.

13 GOOD LUCK EGYPTIAN TALISMANS

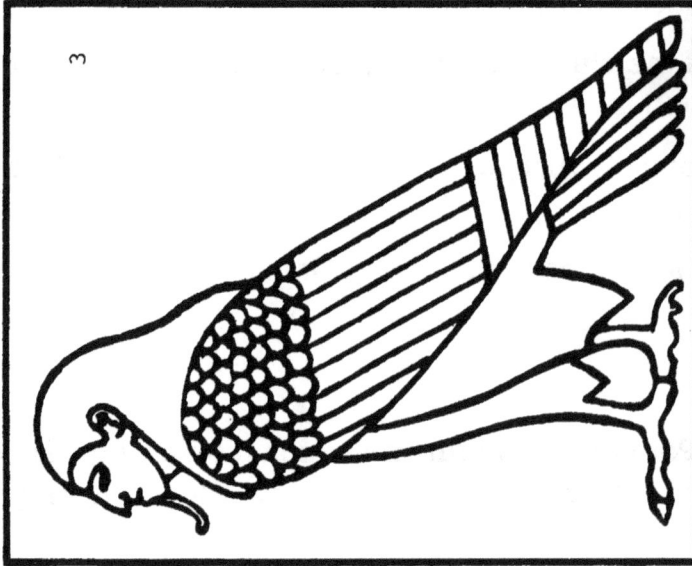

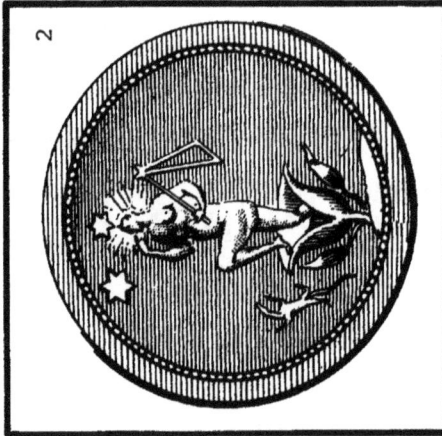

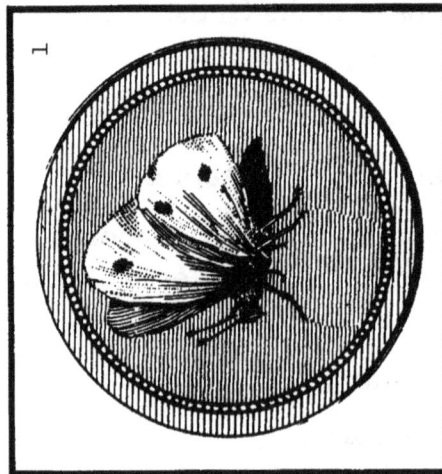

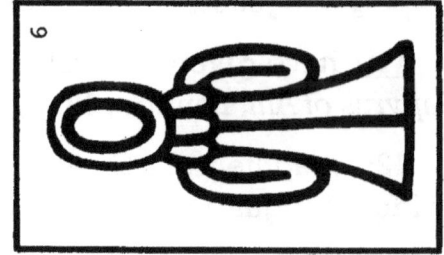

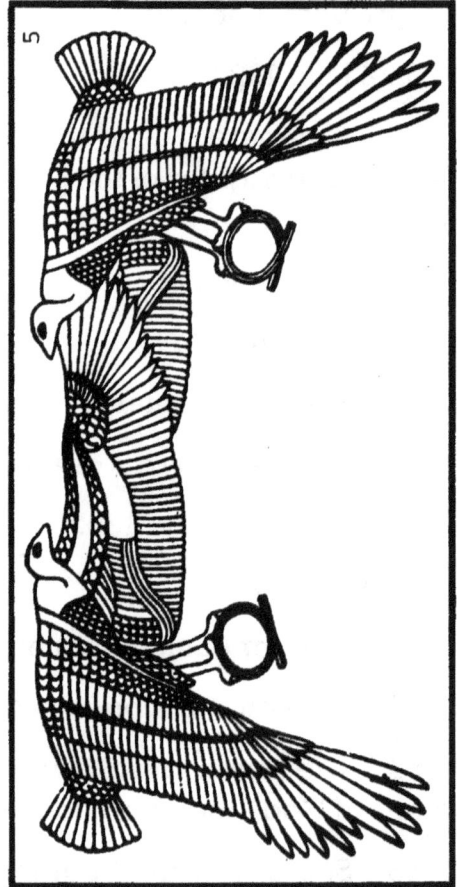

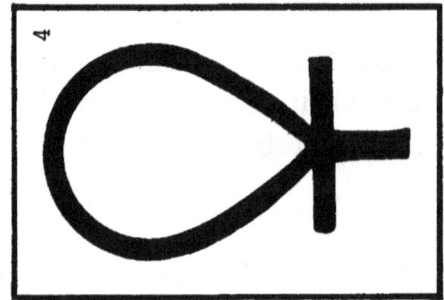

FOR BEST RESULTS COPY THESE TALISMANS ONTO HEAVY COVER STOCK OR PARCHMENT.

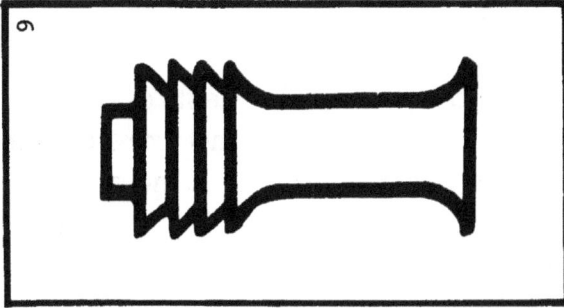

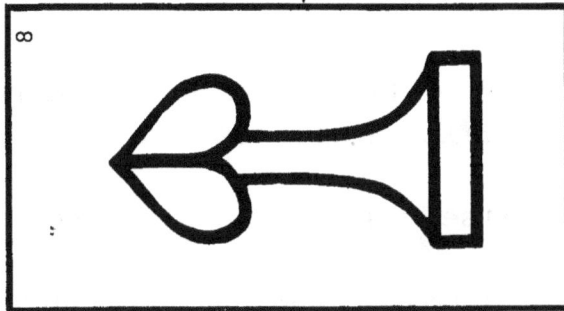

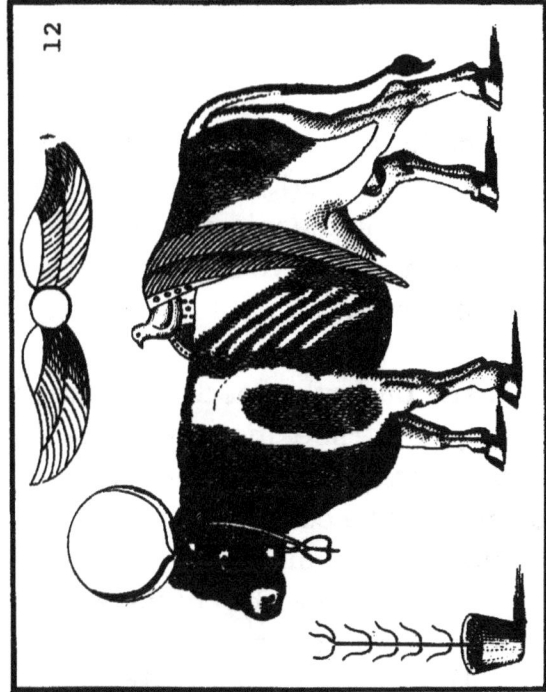

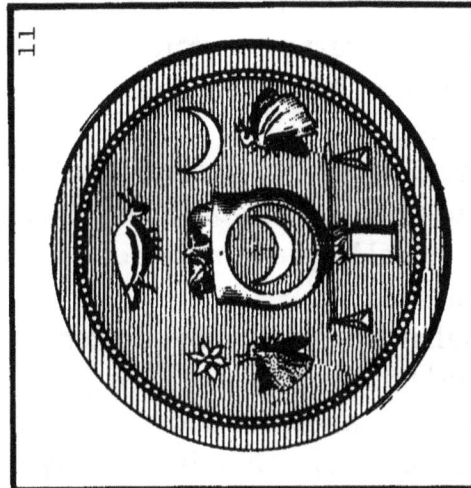

FOR BEST RESULTS COPY THESE TALISMANS ONTO HEAVY COVER STOCK OR PARCHMENT.

THE PYRAMIDS SPEAK

13 GOOD LUCK EGYPTIAN TALISMANS

The talismans on the previous pages were used by the High Priests of Egypt to protect themselves from evil and to attract good luck to those who wore or carried them. Our suggestion is that you cut out these charms and utilize the ones that have the most meaning in your life. Either place them in your wallet or purse or keep them under your pillow for a desireable length of time until you find your life improving.

1. The butterfly stood for "resurrection" and is a charm that should be carried when you are seeking a new direction in your life.

2. This talisman is one of "power" and should be utilized when it is necessary for you to take command of a situation and you must call upon resources that are not normally available.

3. This is the symbol of the soul and may be used when you are searching for spiritual truth or knowledge.

4. The anhk is a universal sign of eternal life and is most oftern carried to attract the good forces of the cosmos.

5. These "vultures" can be of assistance if you feel you have been under psychic attack or have an evil eye cast upon you.

6. Carry the symbol of the "Buckle" if you wish to attract others of like mind and are in need of friendship.

7. The god Criosphinx designates "silence" and should be carried when you suspect others are talking about you behind your back.

8. SAM represents physical love and may be carried to bring you into contact with a soul mate or potential lover.

9. The TET is a good talisman to carry if you wish to build a "tower" of success. Excellent for business and finances.

10. Papyrus bundle springs anew for a love affair that has gone sour.

11. If you are being attacked by enemies, this symbol will brig them to their knees with strong protection.

12. The Apis Bull and sun dial means Providence shines on you. Carry this talisman as a symbol of good fortune.

13. The Scarabeau will bring you freedom from want, and great personal wealth, or so the High Priests contended. See if they were right!

WARNING: The publishers cannot guarantee what these talismans may or may not be able to accomplish. The wearer acknowledges that he or she carries them at their own risk.

THE PYRAMIDS SPEAK

Some Prominent Pyramids From Around The World

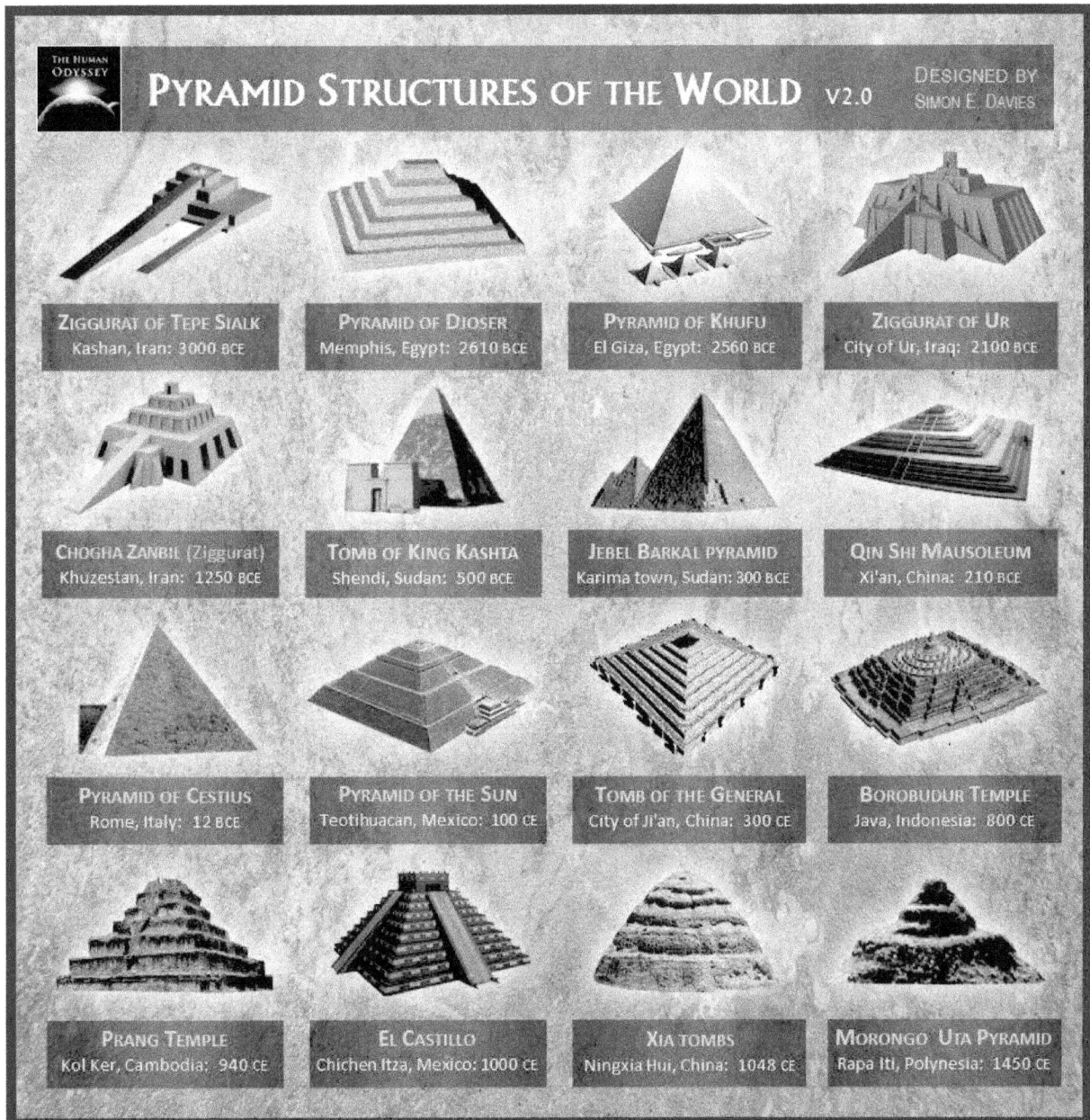

PYRAMID STRUCTURES OF THE WORLD V2.0

THE HUMAN ODYSSEY

DESIGNED BY SIMON E. DAVIES

ZIGGURAT OF TEPE SIALK
Kashan, Iran: 3000 BCE

PYRAMID OF DJOSER
Memphis, Egypt: 2610 BCE

PYRAMID OF KHUFU
El Giza, Egypt: 2560 BCE

ZIGGURAT OF UR
City of Ur, Iraq: 2100 BCE

CHOGHA ZANBIL (Ziggurat)
Khuzestan, Iran: 1250 BCE

TOMB OF KING KASHTA
Shendi, Sudan: 500 BCE

JEBEL BARKAL PYRAMID
Karima town, Sudan: 300 BCE

QIN SHI MAUSOLEUM
Xi'an, China: 210 BCE

PYRAMID OF CESTIUS
Rome, Italy: 12 BCE

PYRAMID OF THE SUN
Teotihuacan, Mexico: 100 CE

TOMB OF THE GENERAL
City of Ji'an, China: 300 CE

BOROBUDUR TEMPLE
Java, Indonesia: 800 CE

PRANG TEMPLE
Kol Ker, Cambodia: 940 CE

EL CASTILLO
Chichen Itza, Mexico: 1000 CE

XIA TOMBS
Ningxia Hui, China: 1048 CE

MORONGO UTA PYRAMID
Rapa Iti, Polynesia: 1450 CE

The city of Ur was one of the most important Sumerian city states in ancient Mesopotamia during the 3rd millennium BC. One of best preserved and most spectacular remains of this ancient city is the Great Ziggurat of Ur. The Great Ziggurat, which is today located in the Dhi Qar Province, in the south of Iraq, is a massive step pyramid measuring 64 m in length, 46 m in width, and 30 m in height.

The Moon God Nanna at the Ziggurat at Ur

THE PYRAMIDS SPEAK

THE PYRAMIDS SPEAK

THE PYRAMIDS SPEAK

THE PYRAMIDS SPEAK

THE PYRAMIDS SPEAK

THE PYRAMIDS SPEAK

THE PYRAMIDS SPEAK

THE PYRAMIDS SPEAK

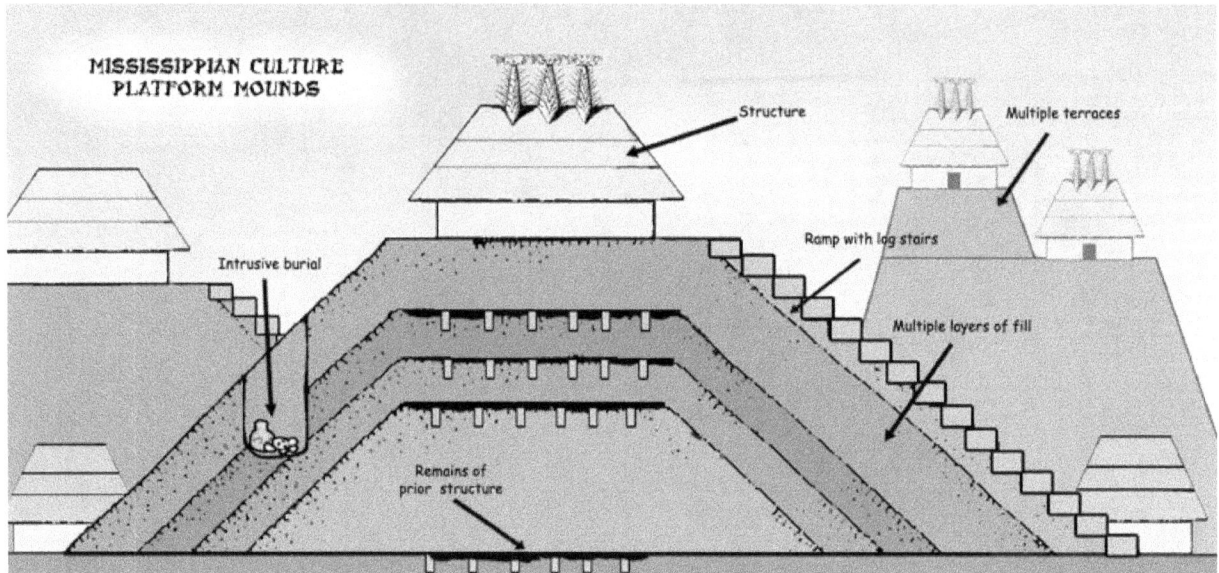

THE PYRAMIDS SPEAK

THE PYRAMIDS SPEAK

THE PYRAMIDS SPEAK

THE PYRAMIDS SPEAK

PYRAMIDS, ENIGMATIC WALLS, CARGO CULTS AND A MYSTERIOUS GLOBAL CIVILIZATION

By Olav Phillips

The Egyptian pyramids are one of the most enigmatic series of structures in the ancient world. They are odd not only because of the sheer scale of their construction, or the apparent celestial alignment to the Orion constellation, but more importantly because they are not alone.

One of the earliest known buildings constructed in the world is in fact a series of simple, but low, pyramid structures found in France called "The Tumulus of Bougon." Constructed in 4700 B.C., these simple pyramids are thought to have served as burial mounds and some of the structures have been found to house more than 200 skeletons.

The structure is simple but demonstrated an obvious early design for a step pyramid. Other Tumulus's found in France, dating to the same time period, such as the Tumulus of St. Michael, also demonstrate this notion of mound building or simple pyramidal design. The question is where did the design come from?

THE PYRAMIDS SPEAK

It was 2600 B.C., nearly 2000 years later, that a mysterious pyramid was constructed in present day Peru at Caral. Meanwhile in Egypt during the same time period there is a massive explosion of pyramid construction. Over the next 100 years the Pyramid of Meidum, the "Bent" Pyramid, the Red Pyramid, The Great Pyramid, the Pyramids of Khafe, Userkaf, Sahure, Neferefre, Niuserre, Djedkate-Isesi, Unas, and Teti are all built. Between 2580 B.C. and 2330 B.C. some 12 major pyramids are constructed in Egypt alone. Over the next few hundred years several more pyramids are constructed but never at the rate or sheer size of these pyramids. All in all some 135 pyramids have been discovered over the last century in Egypt alone.

Then a long unexplained pause takes place. Almost 500 years after the construction of Caral and the Egyptian pyramid complexes there is another pyramid construction boom, only this time in the Kushite kingdoms of Nubia. The pyramids of the Nubia and Kushite kingdoms look strikingly similar in design to the Egyptian pyramids, with the main difference being scale but not design. The Kushite pyramids, while smaller, are almost a perfect match to the Egyptian pyramids. Over the next 600 years the Nubian Kingdoms would construct some 255 pyramids and funerary complexes.

This is where the story gets interesting. At this point in time the construction of step pyramids seems to go global and we start to see pyramids crop up across Asia, even stretching all the way into the Americas. Main points of pyramid concentration appear to be China, South America, then Central America and well into North America. At this point, around 300 B.C., we now appear to have a worldwide phenomenon emerging. But as quickly as the pyramid construction boom started, it mysteriously stops again.

So the question of the hour is why the sudden rapid expansion? The only logical answer seems to be some sort of global communication, be it a trading network or more likely some sort of global enculturation process which established the pyramid as the predominate form of sacred structure. That notion was carried from locale to locale and was introduced from culture to culture, part of a process which appears to have emerged around the 3000 B.C. time period.

The logic around dating the rapid expansion to 3000 B.C. is that the true pyramid design explosion starts in around 3000 B.C. with the massive Egyptian constructions. We then see the collapse of the pyramid culture in Egypt as they start to move underground. It is at that point we see the Nubian pyramids begin to emerge. This would appear to indicate that some sort of contact took place in Egypt prior to the 2600 BCE construction of the great pyramids as well as the mysterious Peruvian pyramid at Caral. That date is significant because it seems to be the ignition point for pyramid use.

102

THE PYRAMIDS SPEAK

So let's assume for the moment that there was some sort of contact between the Egyptians and some unknown cultural group. Why does that make sense? The answer to that question really comes down to the oldest known human-made large-scale structure, the Tumulus of Bougon. The Tumulus is very obviously a step pyramid and it's in France. So what that would appear to indicate is that either the culture which built the Tumulus developed their own design in a pocket or more likely were exposed to the design by some other group. At this point it would appear they were exposed to *something* since millennia later the Egyptians adopted the same design.

Dating the origin of the design and its sacred significance seem to be more difficult. The oldest culture known is in India, and, if the Mahabharata is to be believed, places it some 13,000 years ago. It is at that time that there was a massive conflagration which subsumed that Vedic culture in nuclear fire. But what if there were survivors? Could they have left India in search of other lands? For many years stories have circulated about a lost land called Lemuria which appears to have existed in Pacific Ocean. That would be a logical end point for survivors of a cataclysmic war to start over. It is important to point out that ancient India does provide a design for a sacred structure which is very reminiscent of the step pyramid design.

So what about Lemuria? Conventionally, Lemuria is said to be a massive island which some believe was located deep in the Pacific Ocean. More modern research, principally research performed by the JOIDES Resolution research vessel, seems to point to a sunken super mass in what is now known as the Indian Ocean. The Kerguelen Plateau, as it is now called, was located in the Indian Ocean and occupied a fairly large portion of it. This would be a logical location for a new colony to spring up. It would also explain why the large scale use of pyramids is seen around the Pacific Rim.

What about France? Is it possible that explorers from Lemuria came to Europe via Egypt or the Middle East? Absolutely. We need to remember that the Mahabharata speaks of not only atomic energy but also of flying machines, called Vimanas, which would have made that trip a very easy one from the Indian Ocean.

Lemurians might have explored outwards from the Indian Ocean into Europe and brought their architectural ideas along for the ride. Then perhaps they passed them along to the temple builders in France. This would also explain the sudden disappearance factor, since the knowledge and cultural context would have only been exposed to a limited number of cultures along the way.

So now the question is, why the explosion? It would appear, given the dates involved with various pyramid sites, that the expansion we see is most likely caused by a colonial or cultural expansion. There is no other reasonable explanation for why parallel step pyramids seem to appear from the Nubian Kingdom all the way across the Pacific Ocean into the Americas. This would also explain the mysterious artifact at Yonaguni in Japan.

The pyramid at Yonaguni shows evidence of being a step pyramid in design and measures 490 ft by 130 ft and is about 90 ft tall. It appears to be a smooth construction with walls, platforms, columns, etc., making it very consistent with Mayan pyramids of similar construction. The only issue? It's underwater. This fact originally led Japanese scientist Masaaki Kimura to believe the structure was approximately 10,000 years old. He later revised this estimate to about 3000 B.C., which would place it in the zone of the Egyptian expansion.

This raises an interesting problem. Were those pyramids the result of a cargo cult or more directly caused by the expansion of a heretofore unknown culture? What's interesting is that the very oldest pyramid design was constructed not in Egypt but in France a good 2000 years before the Egyptian pyramid period. It was fairly small, but demonstrated a similar design to the ancient Egyptians. But then it stopped. The design disappeared for the most part and never evolved into massive construction projects. That would seem to indicate this was something the culture had seen and was trying to emulate. Two thousand years later, the Egyptians started major pyramid construction which continued unabated for another 2000 years. In fact, even beyond Egypt, the natives of places like Cahokia in present-day Illinois and other Mississippian cultures built massive earth mounds where their leaders lived.

What's also fascinating is that not only did cultures like the Maya, the Nubian Kingdom and the Aztecs build pyramids, but they also followed some of the same burial practices which involved the burial of significant people in the temple complexes. The dead were given masks of gold or jade, this being dependent on the local material, and buried in elaborate sarcophaguses. This is, however, not true of the Mississippians, who buried their dead differently, indicating either cultural diffusion or cargo cult behavior.

The story then gets stranger. According to popular myth, Lemuria suffered a massive volcanic explosion (sound like Atlantis to anyone?) and sank to the bottom of the ocean. Survivors of the cataclysm are believed to have moved onto various locations along the Pacific Rim, which would also explain the rapid expansion. Some Lemurians are believed to have settled under Mt. Shasta in Northern California.

What's interesting about this idea is that, while there is some evidence of Lemurian activity around Mt. Shasta, mainly strange petroglyphs, artifacts and other myths, there appears to be a new culture which rose up around 1000 A.D. in the same geographic area. This activity could again demonstrate cultural diffusion as generations after the cataclysm new, less knowledgeable, descendents moved outwards from Shasta. This is something history has played out before as a culture rises, then collapses, and during the collapse loses technology which had previously existed.

So what is this mysterious culture? Are these the descendants of the survivors of Lemuria?

In the San Francisco Bay Area, where my journey started, there is a series of mysterious walls that seem to ring the bay. You could imagine that the original unworn walls would have encircled the bay from Fremont all the way to Vallejo then across Marine and on to the Pacific Ocean. The walls also travel inland and appear to ring Mt. Diablo, which is one of the dominate land structures of the area. But that is not the only structure.

In the Sutter Buttes, the walls appear to extend out from the central feature and do indeed look like property divisions with fairly small areas enclosed by larger areas.

In many ways it looks much like county lines but on a micro-scale. This seems to indicate they would have been defensive or property boundaries, but the issue here is boundaries for whom? That is the true question here.

This is especially interesting because the structures themselves seem to cross the boundaries of known indigenous groups and in some cases cross the boundaries between groups which had historically held a high level of animosity towards each other. This would also seem to discount the notion that native groups built these walls since it would require a level of cross cultural collaboration which did not exist, as far as archeology knows.

What has emerged from this exploration is the possibility of a heretofore unknown, large scale, and distributed culture. There appears to be several fairly large population centers where the walls seem to concentrate and divide less land while in other lower population density areas there seem to be larger chunks of land divided up. This can be seen in the Sutter Butte complex vs. Burney Rock Lines. In the Northern area there seems to be another large complex in the area surrounding Mt. Shasta which would be consistent with Shasta being the cultural epicenter and source point.

The interesting thing about the distribution of these large complexes is that they seem to exist around large landmasses and to ring them. This would be comparable to the other pyramid complexes in history, the main difference being the use of a large landmass such as a mountain as opposed to building a pyramid. A large tall structure is used, but, in the absence of a pyramid, they appeared to use a mountain.

Another interesting element of this culture appears to be the propensity to ring bodies of water. This is seen at the Hog Hill location as well as in the Shasta complex.

So the fifty million dollar question is who built this? It would appear to be a distributed group since the construction technique is similar as well as the position of the geographic zones (around hills), with large concentrations around larger landmasses such as mountains then smaller groups around lower hills.

Who built these is something which could be open for debate, but it would seem that, with such a geographic distribution, the ancient Chinese would need to be ruled out since their fleet would not provide the population size for such a level of construction. The apparent age, based on samples examined from the East Bay Wall, would rule out European incursion since the samples inspected would indicate a settlement pattern predating the Spaniards by hundreds of years. It is also important that the relative age estimate is older than 400 years, but, based on conversations, the actual age is probably more in the 500- to 600-year range and maybe even older. Further analysis is needed before a better dating of the rocks can be done.

This ancient, potentially pre-contact, civilization could also account for the persistent stories of Lemurians and survivors of Mu landing in California post-cataclysm. There are stories dating back some time which seem to recall survivors of a great cataclysm settling in California, especially around Mt. Shasta, which also appears to have the highest density of these mysterious walls.

Whether the walls were built by Lemurians or some other ancient pre-contact culture, this would appear to be the source of the story and begs for better and more definitive research to be done. It represents a massive failure on the part of conventional archeology to not investigate an anomaly of this magnitude.

What we can see is a large population, geographically dispersed, which had a fairly sophisticated concept of resource division as well as defense. But what is really interesting is the apparent lack of ruins in these areas. We can see the walls, we can see the concentrations, but there don't seem to be any other ruins. This would suggest either extreme antiquity, meaning the ruins of the settlements are buried, or that, while this apparent civilization did build walls on a massive scale, their structures were temporary or at least made out of non-stone/non-age resistant material. The third possibility is that the walls themselves are not the population centers but maybe agricultural centers with the bulk of the population living in settlements close by.

What we do know is that they are artificial and thoughtfully designed. The evidence also seems to be the final link in the chain of a very old story dating back some 13,000 years and ties together a number of diverse cultures. There seems to be some cargo cult behavior around the Tumulus in France, but also more thought out and directed construction in other areas. You could even argue the mysterious Northern California wall builders or the Chokians were exhibiting cargo cult behavior, but I don't think the same can be said of the Maya, Aztecs and Egyptians.

The true story of the Pyramid Builders may be buried in the past, but we can see the faint traces of a worldwide culture emerge. Periods of expansion and collapse tell that story: the growth of pyramid complexes starting to form in waves across the globe, then dissolving into dust and leaving only the faint glimmer of their former glory.

What this story teaches us is that we need to take a new look at the distribution of these complexes and start to search for patterns in their distribution and for significant cultural similarities. Archeology needs to revisit the pyramid story and honestly reassess it. Until that happens, the true nature of the pyramids around the globe will be mysterious and lost to time.

THE HOUSE OF THE GODS

By Stephen J. Ash

* What was the real purpose of the Great Pyramid of Egypt?

* Was it the burial place of the Pharaoh or something else entirely?

* Did it have any connection to extraterrestrials or something altogether stranger?

* Was the Great Pyramid the House of the Gods?

WHAT WE KNOW ABOUT THE PYRAMID

The Great Pyramid of Cheops is one of the most mysterious places in the world. The pyramid itself is divided into three chambers; the lowest of these is subterranean and lies at the foundations of the pyramid. It was once thought a secret passage ran from there to a door between the paws of the sphinx, constituting a ritual entrance to the pyramid, but this has never been confirmed. Above it, near the center of the pyramid, lies what archeologists call the Lower Chamber, more popularly known as the Queen's Chamber. Immediately above this is the King's Chamber, or Upper Chamber, once thought to have been the burial place of the Pharaoh due to a broken sarcophagus found there. The King's body has never been found, however, leading some to suspect it is hidden somewhere else in the complex. Others suggest it was never there in the first place and that the pyramid served some other purpose, perhaps a ritual or occult one. In 1998, a French team, using the controversial technique of microgravity, which is said to measure local variation in the gravity field, claimed to have detected a new chamber just beneath the Lower Chamber, which would put it at the dead center of the pyramid (taking the subterranean chamber into account). This has been speculated as the real burial place of the Pharaoh by the French group. But many archeologists are skeptical of this (Siliotti, Alberto (1997). Guide to the Pyramids of Egypt; preface by Zahi Hawass.).

THE PYRAMIDS SPEAK

THE REAL NATURE OF THE MYSTERIOUS "AIR VENTS"

Another long-standing mystery of the pyramid is the presence of so called "air channels," thin tunnels running from the interiors of some chambers to the outside walls of the pyramid. While these were first thought of as ventilation shafts, this is no longer believed to be the case because the channels in the Lower Chamber do not appear to reach the outside. Neither do any of the other pyramids have such channels either; in fact, the whole structure of the Great Pyramid is rather unique. Officially, they remain a mystery, but a view receiving increasing evidence is that they are linked to the stars. The King's Chamber contains two channels one in the south wall and one in the north wall. The southern channel emerges directly above the two boat pits located near the pyramid that are said to contain the "sky vessels" the dead Pharaoh was thought to sail in. But, more significantly, it is directly aligned to the belt of the constellation Orion. This is interesting given that the whole Giza complex has been said to be a microcosm of these stars on Earth, though this is highly controversial (http://www.ianlawton.com/oc8.htm)

What cannot be doubted is that Orion was very important to the Egyptian religion and associated with the God Aser, or Osiris, who was linked to the concept of the Pharaoh in the Underworld. Thus the channels may be associated with a belief in the Pharaoh's postmortem survival. The channel in the northern wall is more mysterious, as it seems to be aligned to the Pole Star at the time of the pyramids construction 4500 years ago, Thuban or Alpha Draconis, in the constellation of Draco. This star was also very important to the Egyptians and regarded as the ruler of the fixed stars of the pole, which never set and were called the Ikhemusek, meaning "imperishable ones" or "ancient ones" (Richard H. Wilkinson, The Complete Gods and Goddesses of Ancient Egypt).

The mythical associations with Thuban are uncertain and would have changed with time. In the most ancient Egyptian texts its constellation Draco was associated with a dark goddess, seen as both a primal deity of birth and a destructive aspect of Hathor, in the form of a hippopotamus, similar to the "dragon demon" Tiamat, also linked to the same constellation in Babylon. Later it became associated with Osiris's enemy Set, or with this same dark goddess in conflict with Set, but, by the time the pyramids were built, Heru or Horus was associated with some of these stars as the guardian against the powers of Set. In Babylonia, Thuban was linked to the God Anu, the protector of Order against Chaos, and it was regarded as the House of the Annunaki (familiar to the fans of the Reptilian mythos!); it seems likely in this context, however, that Thuban is linked to myths of Horus.

A JOURNEY TO THE STARS

A common interpretation is that the dead Pharaoh's souls depart through these channels and join the stars, as described in the Pyramid Texts (Allen, James. The

THE PYRAMIDS SPEAK

Ancient Egyptian Pyramid Texts). Apparently his Ba, or active soul, merged with Osiris in Orion and his Ab, or mind soul, traveled to the House of the Gods, where it was judged and either transfigured or eaten by the demon Ammit, "devourer" or "soul-eater" with a body that was part lion, hippopotamus and crocodile. All of this was normally thought of as occurring in the Underworld but had obvious associations with the northern stars (see the Egyptian Book of the Dead).

But was this what the pyramid was really for? There is very little evidence for it at all; no body has ever been found other than the empty sarcophagus, which may have had a ritual purpose. The stellar associations and what we know about the Egyptian religion do fit it rather well. But, even if this was one use, it need not be the only one.

STRANGE HIDDEN CHANNELS IN THE LOWER CHAMBER REVEALED

Because of this association, when two hidden 'channels' were found in the Queen's Chamber they were given a similar association. Although neither of these passages seemed to go as far as the outer wall of the pyramid, they were calculated as aligned to Sothis or Sirius in the south and Kochab in the north. The first was one of the most important stars in the Egyptian belief system, its helical rising linked to the flooding of the Nile and the calendar. Initially linked to a protective Nile God or Goddess, Septu or Sept, it was later associated with Horus and Isis. However, in this context, it also had another association with the jackal headed Anubis, the guide of Osiris (the jackal being symbolically linked to Sirius as the dog was for the Greeks). Kochab is a more obscure connection but a very important one. Archeologists have discovered the pyramid itself is aligned perfectly to the north, though its northern wall is not perfectly geographically aligned. The mythological references here are obscure, but again some associate this star Kochab with Horus. Curiously, in Jewish texts, Kochab is the name of the fallen angel who taught mankind astronomy (see the Book of Enoch), while other sources say he is among the holiest angels. For the Mormons, Kochab is the location of the planet Kolob, the "dwelling place of God." Maybe there is some extraterrestrial intelligence involved here?

MYSTERY OF THE "AIR VENTS" REVEALED

These "air vents" themselves are not, as some New Agers imply, straight tunnels pointing at the stars; their courses make several zigzag turns. Light could not pass down them and they would be useless for sighting the stars, as others have claimed. Meanwhile, the Lower Chamber tunnels make right-angled turns and do not seem to reach the sides. According to robots sent along them, they are blocked by mysterious doors that some believe hide other chambers and others believe are purely symbolic. It is certainly strange that these channels were hidden in the Lower Chamber. But the general consensus is that they are symbolic links to the stars, regardless of whether there are other chambers there or not. What could the stellar connection really be about if it wasn't a cult of the dead?

A RADICAL NEW PICTURE OF THE FUNCTION OF THE PYRAMID

There has been much speculation about the function of the pyramid, some of it interesting, some of it crazy. One popular idea is to connect it to the UFO mystery in some way and even the idea of alien visitors. But today serious UFOlogy has gone through a revolution and few follow the old ETH paradigm, which doesn't seem tenable anymore in the 21st century. That said, mankind has long interacted with Intelligences from the beyond, some of which came in Flying Saucers while others appeared in the triangle drawn by Occults. Was the Great Pyramid the first magic triangle through which these beings made contact with the Egyptian elite?

A POSSIBLE RITUAL CENTER

One thing that always struck me while researching this mystery is that, although there may be something to the Pharaonic Theory, things might also work the other way. The energy may not be flowing out of the pyramid but rather into it. The pyramid is very unique, larger than most others, with a more elaborate arrangement of inner chambers. A notable thing about these chambers is their very high ceilings, which also give them a sonorous acoustic quality. Voices reverberate here in a way perfect for ritual. The atmosphere is intense (both observations from personal contact). The channels in the Upper Chamber could actually serve as ventilation as well as being aligned, allowing people to reside there for long periods. In fact, today a fan is installed in them for that purpose. Could it have actually been a ritual center, with the stellar influence of the Deities coming down the channels into the different chambers? It would be here that they could manifest to their worshipers. The pyramids were sometimes referred to as the Houses of the Gods, so were they thought of as literally living there and contactable? It's an intriguing thought and one never much explored before.

Whether these Gods were really supernatural deities is open to question, and, if they were, perhaps they were illusions faked by the priesthood. We know they had all sorts of tricks and devices for maintaining their power in this way. Or were Other Intelligences, physical or nonphysical, really involved? Perhaps beings from another world? We can reject the idea of real Deities on the one hand and nuts-and-bolts aliens on the other I think. But the in-between notion of powerful non-physical intelligences manifesting through esoteric practice may be a lot more likely. Was the Great Pyramid really the House Of The Gods?

Perhaps, and maybe MUCH MORE, as this work reveals!

THE PYRAMIDS SPEAK

REMEMBERING BILL COX

During his lifetime of achievements, Bill Cox authored many published books and articles which have appeared in numerous international journals. He also served as founder and chief editor of the "The Pyramid Guide," an immensely popular bimonthly newsletter published for nearly a decade. Along with his British-born wife, Davina, he traveled extensively worldwide, presenting self-discovery training workshops on a variety of linear and nonlinear scientific subjects. In addition, for twenty years Bill and Davina traveled throughout the United States and other countries, helping clients and lecturing on the ancient science of Feng Shui. And, while Bill has passed onto the next world, Davina continues the projects he was so dedicated to. She can be reached by email at information@dowsing.com and by postal mail at Fine Media International, P.O. Box 30305, Santa Barbara, CA 93130.

Tim Beckley Remembers His Old Friend, Bill Cox

Though the archaeological community bitterly denies it, I realized as far back as the mid-1970s that ancient pyramids literally ring the earth. My primary sources for this sensational bit of wisdom were my friend Bill Cox, editor of the highly respected *Pyramid Journal,* as well as a gentleman who I met under somewhat unusual circumstances.

During a trip out to the old Giant Rock Airport in the Mojave Desert – site of the famous UFO/New Age conclaves of the 1950s and 60s that attracted thousands to hear the latest news on our space visitors – Bill treated me to his wisdom and knowledge regarding the placement of pyramids at strategic locations across the globe. With this data in hand, Bill and I both concluded it might be possible to uncover still additional pyramid structures that would otherwise be lost to the sands of time.

But why were these "unidentified and unacknowledged pyramids" placed so strategically? Why wouldn't they just "pop up" here and there at the whim of the cultures that built them?

"The spherical line of pyramids around the world was so designed in order to channel higher energies for power and for use in certain directions by high priests and the elite of prehistoric civilizations," was the basic conclusion that Bill came to concerning this matter. Bill Cox's insight has been invaluable throughout this book and we only wish he were still here to converse with us and to pass along additional information that might have been discovered in the years since his passing.

The Pyramids: Their Hidden Supernatural Meanings And Capabilities

By Bill Cox

FOREWORD

I came into this study sometime around 1968, not necessarily as a skeptic, but as one who really didn't know the meaning of the word "psychic" or other terms used by people investigating paranormal phenomena.

I once had an experience which might have been a sighting or a UFO contact. I was coming back from

The late Bill Cox and Davina Cox in Japan.

Guadalajara, Mexico, one night in 1969, driving across the flat desert near El Centro, California, at about 11 p.m. I suddenly saw, up ahead and to my right, what looked like a welding torch. I watched this bright light with fascination because it became larger than any welding torch flare I had ever seen. It would first pulsate from brightness to dimness, becoming ever larger and brighter, until it lit up the night sky like twilight. It lasted for about a minute, reaching a maximum level and blinding my eyes before it pulsated down into a dim glow. Then it held steady for a moment before completely vanishing. It looked like a globe, a London street lamp. After that event, my life underwent many rapid changes.

In 1972, I began publishing the "The Pyramid Guide." The newsletter's main focus was the realm of higher energies, exploring sources of free energy anti-gravity psychic phenomena such as dowsing, psychometry, mediumship, astral travel and so on. Over the course of 10 years, I received thousands of letters from all over the world in which people told of having experiences that cannot be explained through ordinary physical scientific investigation.

We are dealing with unusual persons and events on a planetary scale and at an ever increasing and accelerated pace. It is becoming more commonplace to see humans demonstrate abilities such as clairvoyance (extended sight), seeing lower into the spectrum (infrared), or higher into the ultraviolet range. Some even go beyond into x-ray vision or night vision. A surprising number of people have acquired some degree of clairaudience. This means people can hear voices and sounds that are perceived from within and are little understood. The voice heard may offer guidance, issue a warning or may be a musical sound. Others develop clairsentience, the ability to feel something at a distance without touching it. I have personally been active in researching and writing about these phenomena, which also include Dowsing and Geomancy.

Although few humans know how to control and make positive use of these gifts, most can be trained to do so. But it requires time, self-discipline and infinite patience under the guidance of a noble and knowledgeable teacher. Exciting research is going on in the world today with the use of biofeedback equipment, the electroencephalograph. By monitoring the brain waves of individuals, we are able to establish that there is some kind of electrochemical change going on in the brain of the person which can be scientifically recorded. Another important line of investigation is split-brain research. Science now knows a lot more about the mind and the brain than ever before. At last, the true value of intuitive cognition can no longer be ignored.

Through my own research, I have become convinced that the mind is separate from the brain. The brain is the computer center, the physical organ that receives, intellectually processes and sends the focused information registering in our sensory apparatus and data from our intuition as well. Thus the mind is not solely the brain. The mind is a field of consciousness that interpenetrates the body and surrounds it. The mind can travel for great distances in an instant and go beyond the barriers of time and space without limitations. It can thus make contact with another mind, or another creature, object or substance in space.

Through split-brain research, we know that the right side of the brain directly serves the intuitive mind and is capable of perceiving objects in space outside the limitations of time. It can see at a distance, perceive and gather knowledge and information beyond that reported in the mind through the ordinary five senses. The left brain is dominated by the clock-time world in which we live. It thrives on logic. Documented evidence now shows that the right brain can perceive and bring through data not ordinarily registering in the left hemisphere. The main goal of this research is the integration of the two hemispheres. This will happen through new learning techniques directed at working with the right side of one's brain and will involve subliminal and supraliminal perceptions. This information, no longer considered zany by progressive scientists, ironically has always been known by the world's great mystics for thousands of years.

What we need today is better equipment to prove that what we already know is intuitively true. Some work is being done in this area. Soon, we'll be hearing more about "subjective physics" and "intuitional instrumentation." These New Age Sciences will be greatly aided by sophisticated photography and better computer and electronic equipment, thus proving to the scientific community that it is possible to communicate with other dimensions and other realms of existence and verify the contact made with physical instruments.

Other relatively new – what are really rediscovered – sciences include psychotronics and psionics (mind over matter), with or without the help of instrumentation respectively. All of the foregoing divisions of ancient and sacred sciences will be most useful in validating the true existence of UFOs and unseen kingdoms, or dimensions coexisting with our own planetary life systems, human, animal, plant or mineral.

PYRAMID REPLICA ALTERS THE AURA

By Bill Cox

Shortly before psychic researcher Verne Cameron made his transition into the beckoning planes beyond, we ran a little test with a twelve-inch square-based pyramid placed atop my head. We wanted to see if the miniature aluminum model of the Great Pyramid would alter the auric fields around my form. Cameron had previously found some astounding alterations in the human aura using cones and carbon magnets.

Before I donned the Pyramid, the Dowsing Master, with his AURAMETER, carefully traced the outer limits of my etheric outline. As expected, the energy field pushed outward from my figure about an inch and one-half in the region above my knees and on up along the arms to shoulder level on each side. A steady field of increased emanations in the head area pushed the AURAMETER's pointer out and away with a pronounced thrust.

Then, placing the replica in position on my head, Cameron checked the earlier measurements. His determinations were as follows:

1. My etheric outline had entirely disappeared.

2. An apparently unknown shaft of energy poured outward from each elbow.

3. Cylindrical-shaped beams raced upward from the apex above my head and downward below my feet. Cameron, with the AURAMETER, found the lower rays going right through the seat of the chair I was standing on. The shafts darted outward, upward and downward, mysteriously suggesting a cross.

THE CAMERON AURAMETER was originally designed as an underground water-locating Dowsing Compass. Because of its extraordinary sensitivity, it has since been used to outline the human aura, form energies and detect remnant psychic vibrations.

ELEVATION LOOKING WEST

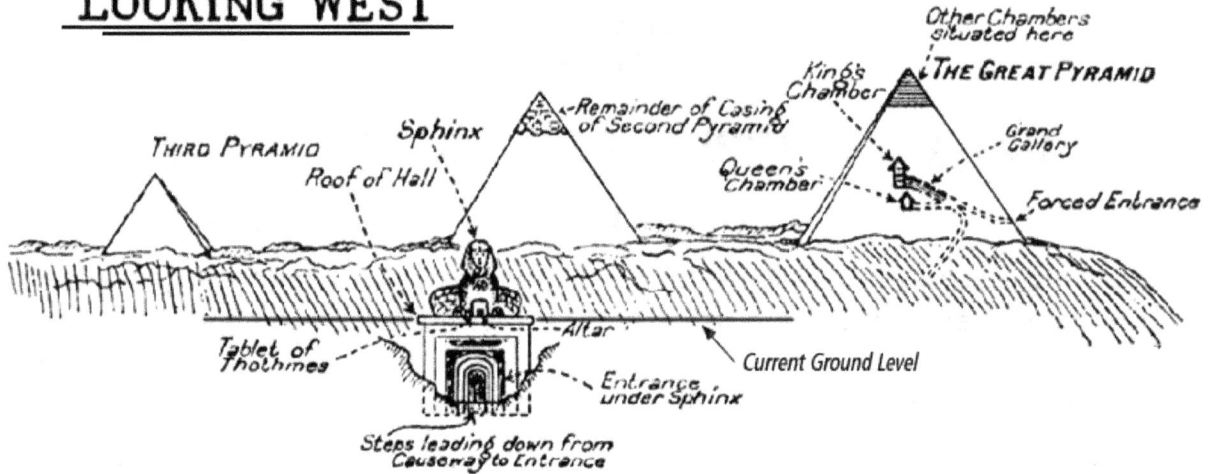

HALF SECTIONAL ELEVATION OF SPHINX, SUBTERRANEAN TEMPLE, CAUSEWAY AND PASSAGES. NOT TO SCALE

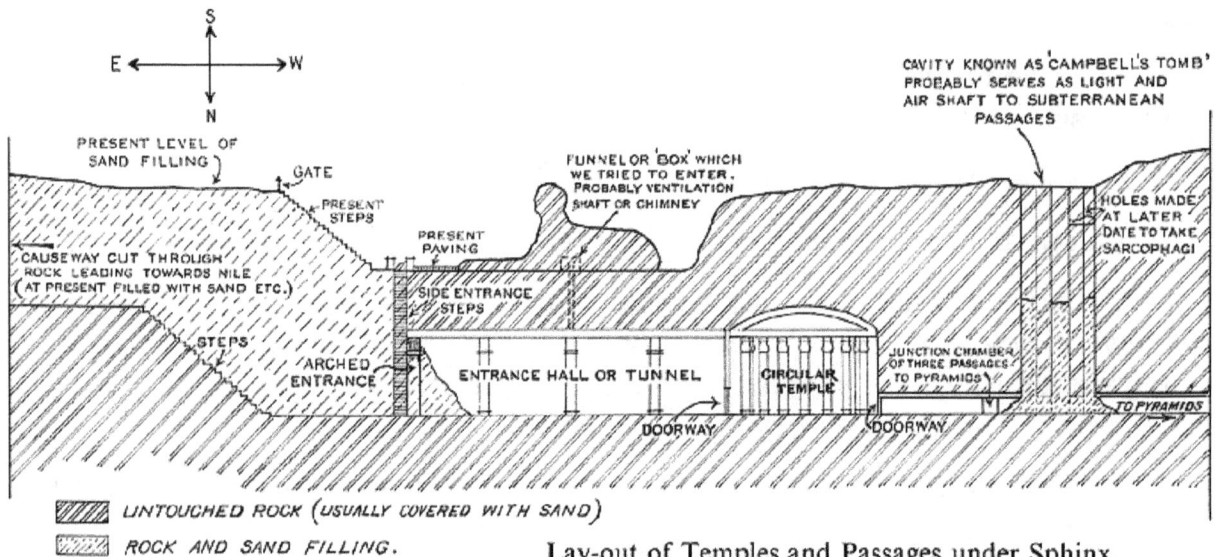

Lay-out of Temples and Passages under Sphinx.

PYRAMID, VOICE-TAPE PHENOMENA

By Bill Cox

A 12' x 12' base pyramid loaned to the late Bill Welch, of Encino, California, by "The Pyramid Guide," doubled the number of spirit voices registered on his reel-to-reel tape recorder. The results of Bill's tape experiments with tonal voice messages from the worlds beyond again substantiates the pyramid's unique qualities in receiving and transmitting higher energies, higher octaves and harmonics.

William Addams Welch, former television and movie writer, was a most patient researcher. After a long period of testing, he was satisfied the pyramid, although not improving the sound level of reception, did appreciably step up the frequency of signals. Bill scientifically proved the authenticity of spirit-voice imprints appearing on unrecorded blanks winding through any commercially-available recorder in a soundless room. "There was a definite drop in the quantity of messages when I removed the replica from atop the recorder," said Bill. "But after three months with the pyramid resting on top of my machine, the increase in signals continued, even after the replica had been removed."

For several years, Welch had developed a remarkable collection of taped voices and a variety of chimes, bells and raps. They were usually preceded by a click, rap, breath or word cue, but, even after a decade of research, the unexpected occurred at every turn. For example, some messages transcribed at half or double the midway speed of 3% forced him to increase or reduce the playback speed before it became intelligible.

Eighteen outstanding tonal voice imprints of conversational quality were impressed on tape, free of the usually expected static, whispers, tape hiss, inaudibles and other distortions. To his surprise, upon replay two days later, the voices were completely wiped out by some unknown cause. But, curiously, the ordinary external sounds of random nature, such as traffic noise, a barking dog and shifting guests noted on the original playback still remained unerased and unaltered throughout the session. This suggests the possibility of the "other worldly" broadcast being transmitted on ultra-high frequencies, beyond the range of reception by human ears and known electronic equipment's ability to reproduce once-evident audibles. Could the seemingly erased voices still be present on this tape, broadcasting in vibrations outside the range of human perception?

And if one has nagging doubts, consider the types of messages recorded from the so-called "other side." Advice and accurate information spoken by the voices came through about people Bill and his guests knew who had passed on. These communications were apparently initiated by skilled technicians living in a much higher state of vibration and intellectual development, far beyond our own here on earth. Their world allegedly lies in dimensions outside the etheric and astral planes interpenetrating and surrounding Earth. "They have devised their own means of coming through," said Bill. "It's their test results, not mine. There's little I could do that I wasn't already doing at my end. As they improved their techniques, I began to get better reception. Sometimes they offered suggestions I could try and we had our failures . . ." Bill could often hear these other worldly scientists discussing among themselves other means of approach, as though he was eavesdropping on a conversation filtering through a wall from a distant chamber.

For verification, Bill questioned them in cross-correspondence using the old standby, automatic writing. The answers were often verified, as for example, with the sudden improved quality of reception when the Arizona couple was present. "It showed how difficult it was to work within universal laws without a full understanding of their correct application," said Bill.

"Progress has to be gradual," he continued. "Yet, I've had some of this country's best mediums in here and there was no noticeable improvement in the quantity or quality of voice-tape contacts. So if this is a mediumistic phenomenon, where are we?"

Signals were often weak. Sometimes a single word required patient listening and interpretation. At other times, phrases, sentences and even whole paragraphs poured through. There were moments when atmospheric disturbance was stronger than the voices. (Experienced voice-tape researchers prefer night reception over daytime tuning.) Bill believed that a computerized filtering process might offer some solutions for clarity of listening.

Bill went on to explain. "These are highly evolved people who at one time experienced life in the Earth plane. They have had to lower the frequencies of their own bodies as much as possible to reach us, and it's no simple task," he added. "They want earth people to be comfortable with, and assured of, the expectation of certain survival beyond physical death."

THE GREAT PYRAMID AND REPLICAS:
ALL THINGS TO ALL PEOPLE

By Bill Cox

The Great Pyramid can be compared with the sun. It is an instrument of life, power and the deeper mysteries. Ask various members of a group: "What does the sun give you?" Answers will be diverse, yet correct. One replies: "The sun lights the world; it enables me to see." Another answers: "The sun warms me." Still another comments: "The sun makes things grow – you know – photosynthesis in plants, etc." The next exclaims: "The sun is a great electromagnet; without it, there would be no electromagnetism, radio, global or other energies." And finally: "The sun is the control key in our solar system; it keeps Earth and our nearby planets in orbit."

Now, the Great Pyramid surely belongs in a category with the sun. Readers, writers, researchers, students, visitors, guests and travelers repeatedly tell us this greatest of all the world's Seven Wonders is an ancient "time capsule." Enclosed within its diverse stone blocks, passageways, chambers and measurements, in its precise location, orientation and outer structural form, one seeks the key to the mysteries and wisdoms of the ages. It is, according to pyramidologists, a record of the history of mankind on this planet, containing exact information relating to the unknown and known (Biblical) past, a chronology of significant events encompassing the present, ancient prophecy and the future prospects of mankind's evolutionary growth or downward slide into technological oblivion and/or survival in the New Age.

The Great Pyramid and replicas of it are alchemical instruments, changing both organic matter (mummification, dehydration and preservation) and so-called inorganic matter (sharpening metals, affecting electronic devices, etc.) in beneficial ways. It energizes plants so they grow faster, better, attaining higher essence, ad infinitum. The Great Pyramid is also a temple of meditation, initiation and rejuvenation. It is made up of two and a half million stone blocks. This great monument is a master slide-rule, computer, and a mathematical wonder.

PLAN OF THE PYRAMIDS
— AND SPHINX —
AS ORIGINALLY BUILT

·SHOWING·
the open Causeway
and the subterranean Temple & Passages,
from an original sketch by Piazzi.

CAUSEWAY, TEMPLE & PASSAGES NOT TO SCALE

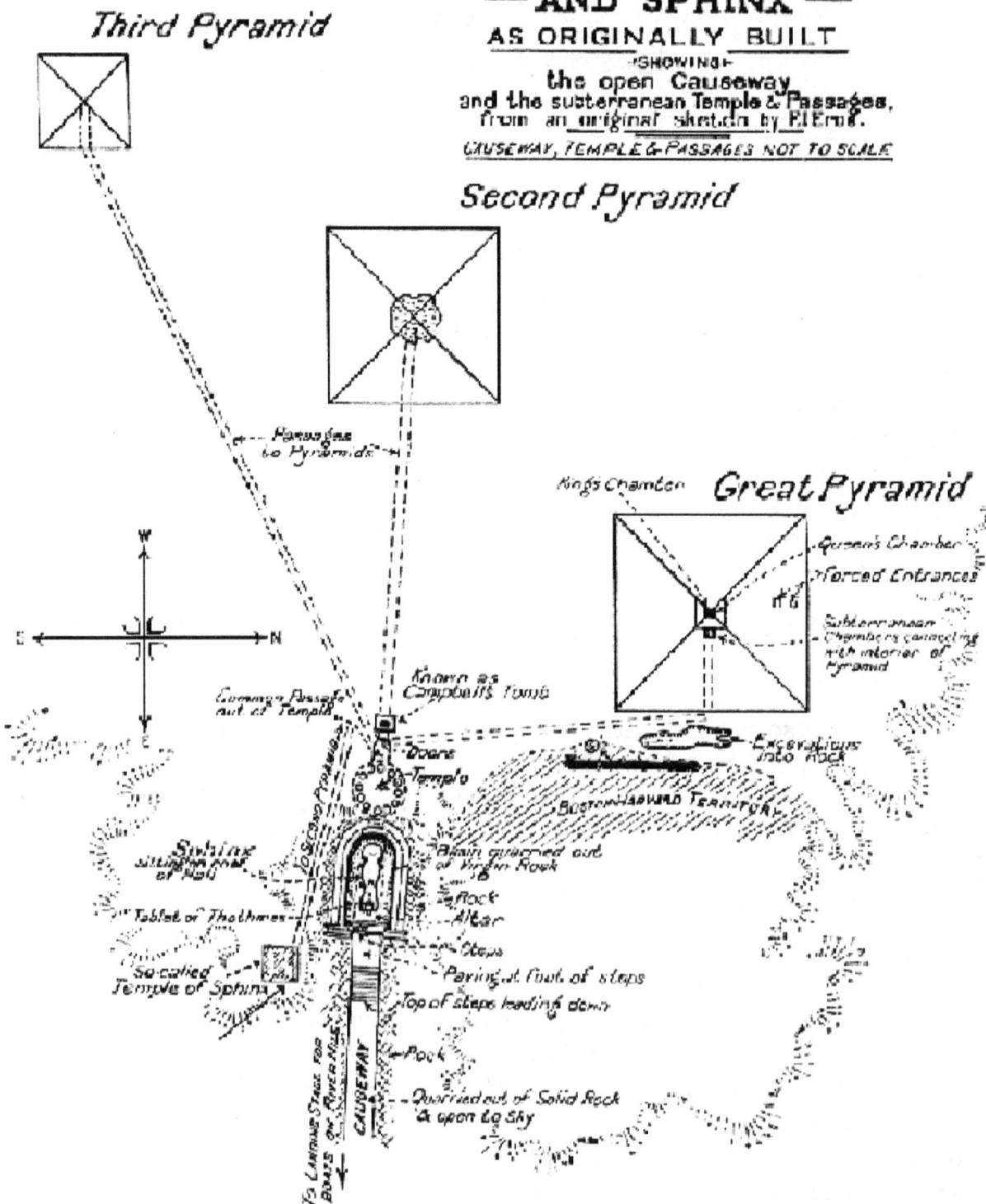

Third Pyramid

Second Pyramid

Great Pyramid

King's Chamber

Queen's Chamber

Forced Entrances

Subterranean
Chambers connecting
with interior of
Pyramid

Passages
to Pyramids

W

E — N

Common Passage
out of Temple

Known as
Campbell's Tomb

Doors

Temple

Sphinx
sitting on mass
of Rock

Tablet of Thothmes

So-called
Temple of Sphinx

Basin quarried out
of Virgin Rock

Rock
Altar

Steps

Paving at foot of steps

Top of steps leading down

Rock

Quarried out of Solid Rock
& open to Sky

Excavations
into Rock

Boston-Harvard Territory

To Landing Stage for
Boats on River Nile

CAUSEWAY

PYRAMIDS, EVIDENCE OF HIGHER BEINGS
FROM OUT OF THE PAST

By Bill Cox

During several expeditions to Egypt, I learned that what Egyptologists and archaeologists tell us isn't always unquestionable fact. Unfortunately, their conclusions are based upon the examination of artifacts, dead bodies and bones – anything that can be materialistically verified. The more bones they find, the more they are convinced that Darwin was right in his contention that we are descended from monkeys. If they want to make a monkey out of themselves, it's O.K. with me, but I think we are descended from wise forefathers who evolved from even higher, more advanced civilizations whose material records have been obscured throughout history. Pre-historical, antediluvian research is often difficult to verify because ancient technologies – unlike our modern, objective sciences – were of a subjective nature. Today we refer to this phenomenon as "Parascience."

Our technology is totally dependent upon our senses for verification. It so often denies the subjective aspect, the fact that we can often verify outer world data by going within. The method of dating is continually being revised. The idea that higher man emerged only four to five thousand years ago just isn't so. Some know it isn't so themselves, but few among these scientists are brave enough to admit it. One can find it frustrating going to an Egyptologist or archaeologist with what appears to be a startling new discovery. Since the materialistic scientist is locked in, if it involves something that he must also weigh intuitively along with examining it in orthodox scientific terms, his concrete mind usually rejects the subjective information. Then again, his colleagues might laugh at him. He wants to protect his position. So, there is actually a deliberately perpetrated fraud going on in science today. It is the scientific community that is resisting new knowledge. I've learned – as others have – to generally avoid the problem of unrealized expectations concerning physical scientists. We must go to the intuitive scientists, men and women who think and function on both the inner and outer planes of experience.

THE PYRAMIDS SPEAK

Most humans are capable of contacting and cognizing other modes of intelligence. The gateway is found through one's intuition. The difference between the intellect and the intuition is that, whereas the intellect works with the parts, the intuition sees the whole. We could dismantle a brand new Ford and leave the parts on the shore of New Guinea, and the aborigines would use them as cooking utensils, weapons of warfare, or wear them as ornaments. Not having seen an automobile before, the pile of auto parts would be a wonder to them. We could go back there 10 years later and we wouldn't see an assembled automobile on the shores of New Guinea. Some genius or informed person has to conceive of or understand the nature of the whole, the complete unit. Being limited in scope, the intellect works with parts. It divides to understand. But the wisdom mind (intuition) unites to comprehend things. Understanding then comes from the union of intellect and intuition to conceive the "whole thing."

These ancient higher beings had this ability. When they looked at a work of art or a monument, they saw it in its totality. They were not linear in their thinking. An example of the process involved would be this: when one looks at the Sphinx, one might first see it as a religious object if he were a priest. Perhaps it would be described as an engineering wonder if one were to ask an engineer what he made of the ancient sculpture. Finally, one could look into the philosophy and legends surrounding it. We could eventually synthesize a dozen different processes.

The Sphinx is therefore not limited to one expression, nor is the Great Pyramid. This is why science finds the legends about the pyramids and the ancient Sacred Sciences hard to accept: because no matter what line of study one goes into, one could build a case for it. Since our technology is so linear, it is very difficult to accept the fact that in the past there were wise men within various races of people with the wisdom and intellect to create a monument or a work of art that was all-inclusive, one that embraced the sciences of their time, including religion, philosophy and the anatomy of man. Their greater monuments, designed and constructed with near absolute purpose, remain, for the most part, incomprehensible to the Western mind today.

Scientific prejudice compounds the problem. Curiously, we see and know only what we want to see and know. Humans have that strange gift, to literally tune-out that which is too difficult to cope with or understand, retaining a blind spot regarding the information until some future time when one can handle it. This phenomenon not only tricks one's mind but can blur the vision, dull one's senses and erase from memory valid and useful things concerned with life itself.

Before me lies a chart of optical illusions. As my eyes shift from left to right eye dominance, a cleverly designed (two-dimensional) staircase ascends, is seen as a left-side portal, now right, again left, and so on.

THE PYRAMIDS SPEAK

Another particular arrangement of geometric shapes (designed to trick the eyes) presents two rings surrounded by various patterns and colors. One unmistakably appears larger than the other, but I'm told the circles in the center are of equal dimension. I could compare sizes with a coin to make sure the author isn't trying to fool me, but I know better. His analysis is correct. This isn't the first time my visual apparatus has deceived me.

With some illusory patterns, I cannot contemplate one in its entirety and fully comprehend the design applying ordinary reasoning processes; the eyes insist upon focusing on some particular line, corner or section of it. After studying each particular geometrical form in its part making up the whole, I decide that all lines do lie in their proper perspective and am forced to admit: "Optical illusion strikes again."

The Great Pyramid, the Sphinx, Easter Island statues, Stonehenge and other spectacular world monoliths and megaliths, including ancient pictographs, petroglyphs, hieroglyphs and symbols, may at times also be likened to bona fide optical illusions. We do not see them in their totality as combined scientific, artistic, and religious natural wonders. We invariably try to comprehend them with the intellect, which processes information by division, examining the complete structure according to a scientific, artistic, religious or engineering point of view and then trying to take something of the whole out of its parts. The static mind becomes enraptured with the fragments of effects; the analytical mind proceeds from oneness to the "Wholistic" imprint.

But how does one alter awareness in such a way that the entire design can be simultaneously understood in its totality? There are two powerful avenues of instant cognition available (among others) to any rational mind: Subliminal and Supraliminal Perception.

Meanwhile, one could say multiple-perception is nothing more than scattered, unfocused observation. At one level, this would be a valid criticism, but, in the higher planes of consciousness, omni-perception enables one to contemplate "what is," not "what only appears to be." We may have to study a structure, artwork or scientific object using a systems approach, that is, pursue its purpose and function in series, first in one way, then study it from another standpoint and so on. Then, after careful analysis, try to put all of the impressions together to hopefully understand its full content.

WONDERFUL DISCOVERIES IN EGYPT

By Bill Cox

It has long been known and prophesied that hidden key(s) opening little-known doors to the greater and lesser mysteries in Egypt would be found (one by one) sometime along the cusp of the Aquarian Age. People in ever-increasing numbers the world over feel an unfathomable compulsion, a peculiar magnetic pull or guidance, as it were, to learn and relearn more about the enigma of the pyramids and the Sphinx. Such a group of inspired, inquisitive and well-informed researchers made the long journey to Cairo March 20th, 1979.

The research team included an Egyptologist, Pyramidologist, educators, writers, psychics, alternative healers, business persons, a photographer and supportive, aware investigators. Credit should be given to Mark Singer of Tulsa, Oklahoma, who organized the tour and skillfully orchestrated the talents and personalities of some 22 investigators arriving from coast to coast, border to border, throughout the United States.

All members of the expeditionary force looked forward with heightened expectations that some new and important discoveries would be made. They were made, as proven by our brief closure meeting held on the plane during our return flight from Athens to the U.S.

No one really expected to be the "chosen one" who would roll back the great stone and open the bronze gate leading to the hidden hall of records. This was a reconnaissance mission involving perhaps a hundred or more individual and group tests. The homework had been thoroughly screened. Some researchers had proceeded nearly as far as they could go without further onsite investigation. A few others were making a return visit in order to verify previous information and to keep a watchful eye, alert for new revelations.

The following reports represent only a small part of the trip's unfolding, to be highlighted by continuing research and awaiting publishing or copyright clearance: Using a pitch-pipe, I found that the King's Chamber, the truncated apex (invisible) chamber, and subterranean compartments in the Great Pyramid, all beautifully resonated to the tone of middle "C," located at the center of any piano keyboard.

Two unexpected things happened during the several sound-chamber tests made: (1) An Egyptian guide leading a tour group into the King's Chamber from the antechamber called out: "Listen to my voice. It will ring out like a bell when I chant a certain note." I wasn't too surprised upon checking his intonation with the pitch-pipe. It was a crystal clear, highly resonating "C." (The humble guide had a strong, masterful voice and apparently possessed the gift of absolute pitch.) His outcry caromed off the walls innumerable times, ever increasing in intensity, proving earlier reports by professional musicians and a sound engineer with sophisticated recording equipment that the King's Chamber in the Great Pyramid is a perfect sound chamber. It was, to be sure, purposefully designed and built as a part of a grand schematic makeup of the overall pyramid as one supernal musical instrument of cosmic proportions.

(2) Then, atop the Great Pyramid at night, I again intoned the note "C" on my pitch-pipe. (Other notes registered with surprising resonance but not nearly with the gusto of middle "C.") My personal guide, who had made the climb uncountable times with tourists through the years, was also taken aback by the startling resonance produced by the rather subdued tonal thrust of my tiny pitch-pipe. He said he had never encountered this phenomenon before. Both of us agreed the musical tone rang back as though there were invisible but very real walls enclosing the missing 33 vertical feet pyramidion. I had heard the neumatic, pre-physical capstone still rests up there atop the Great Pyramid (the secret chamber of the Most High, the eye of God, symbolized on the U.S. Dollar bill). But this mini-apartment, lowered down to Earth from heaven, reportedly cannot be viewed by the eyes of the profane; rather, the presumed missing capstone has been there in its invisible state all the time, beheld only by adepts, certain masters and higher initiates who can see into this lofty vault and interpret the knowledge and wisdom of the ages believed encoded there. Can this towering secret pyramidion be the long sought missing Hall of Records?

PYRAMID/EGYPTIAN MYSTERIES:

UNANSWERED QUESTIONS

By Bill Cox

After research expeditions to Egypt, Mexico and South America, one thing stands out above all other considerations: There's at least a partially organized cover-up of vital information that would, if revealed, overturn many basic scientific beliefs about the origin of man.

These disclosures would drastically contradict Darwin's theories on evolution. But, even if revealed, and even if scientific information were suddenly to be made public, with the backing of orthodox scientists, it probably wouldn't be wholly believed anyway. It often takes generations to uproot very old and outdated concepts. Curiously so, the flat earth people are still with us.

In attempting to untangle this strange web of mystery, one continually encounters the following barriers to investigation and verification: Some of the most promising archaeological sites concealing the great mysteries have been kept secret by archaeologists, Egyptologists, and Mayan-ologists. In fact, certain sites have been declared off-limits to other than authorized personnel or carefully screened individuals and groups sympathetic with current and accepted scientific explanations or to those with money who support such projects and authorities with credentials from certain approved institutions. Independent investigators, who usually function outside the perimeter of the foregoing elite, often must scheme to find ways to probe deeper into things in order to access often suppressed and overlooked genuine information.

Then, when the something of value turns up, it is frequently ignored, immediately challenged or quickly dismissed by scientific authority as "sheer nonsense." Various puzzling artifacts, oracles and ancient trappings worn, held by or surrounding priest-kings, queens, initiates and the ancient magi, as depicted in the historic pictographs, petroglyphs and stone statues, are regularly explained away as being only symbols of life, truth, purity and so on. These artifacts are, more often than not, disregarded in text and picture captions dealing with the subject.

Nearly all efforts to scientifically prove that the pyramids and other massive stone structures were built with ropes, logs and hordes of driven slaves, Hollywood style, simply cannot be verified by scientists who support those theories. The world's other great stone megaliths present another case in point.

Based upon the reasonable assumption that flash photography of ancient and fading wall paintings dissipates the quality of detail still evident in the ruins, why are serious researchers prohibited from photographing other ancient artifacts, ruins and certain equipment not so affected? Of course there are inconsiderate shutterbugs that can be annoying. But are the authorities in charge using these incidents as excuses to discourage the inevitable embarrassing questions that arise with photographic documentation?

For example, at the museum in Cairo, the most significant discoveries concerning higher energy research cannot be photographed. One can only hurriedly make sketches. Descriptive captions identifying the subject or object are so often lacking in imagination. Mention is seldom made of their obvious mystical meanings. The museum catalog, along with these identification cards with exhibit number and the usual textbook explanation, leave one hungering for something more than the current offerings. New and proper ways of getting this precious information out must be found, uncovering and exposing the cover-up to whatever degree it may exist.

ANCIENT PYRAMIDS RING THE PLANET

By Bill Cox

Recent discoveries of ocean-floor pyramids in the Atlantic support the theory that a belt of such land and sea structures encircle the globe. This pyramid meridian follows the 30 degrees north latitude arc girdling the earth. It is a notoriously active passage, intersecting some of the world's most significant land and sea borders and historic sites. This track also includes notable regions of magnetic anomalies: the Bermuda Triangle off Florida, the Devil's Sea south of Japan, and the Great Pyramid, that great time-capsule, observatory and library of stone in Egypt.

Knowledgeable researchers believe the larger pyramids of ancient times were likely prime sources for and distributors of energy gathered from the Universe. Their secondary purpose, according to some current textbook theories, came after the pyramids were "adapted" to the culture, religious and burial practices of civilizations that came later.

It now appears these pyramids, marked on a world map or globe at the locations where first constructed, will reveal a secret message. The expected impartation deals with the following observations: 1) The pyramid belt was constructed to reduce earth's wobble on its axis. 2) The spherical line of pyramids around the world was so designed in order to channel higher energies for power to be aimed in certain directions by the high priests and elite of prehistory civilizations. 3) The message also indicates that the pyramid meridian defines the best areas of search for the world's as yet undiscovered and most illuminating antiquities; the time is at hand in the Age of Aquarius, even though earth changes through the millennia have made deserts or ocean bottoms out of many verdant, populated areas along this belt. 4) The moment for New Age "tuning," a time for humankind to tune back into the very core of its inner being, has arrived – a time for the human races to re-tune back into one another, nature and the cosmos.

THE PYRAMIDS SPEAK

Excitement mounts as the eye follows the compass line on the world map east or west of the Great Pyramid of Giza along 30° north latitude. Tracing the line eastward, we find Jerusalem, nearby Sakaka, in northern Arabia, the historic city of Ur, Kuwait in southern Iraq, forming the seat of ancient Mesopotamia, the region of the Babylonian, Assyrian and Sumerian peoples who constructed several pyramidal monuments and ziggurats.

This region of early Mesopotamia meets the junction of the historic, United Rivers, the Euphrates and Tigris waterways, exiting as one in the Persian Gulf near the latitude north 30° line. The pyramid belt continues on across the southern tip of Afghanistan and through Saharanpur, India. The Hindus, in their Puranas, describe pyramids of such antiquity that they no longer exist, predating any known pyramids found on land today

The eastern passage then proceeds through the northern tip of Nepal and onward, dividing the heart-lines of Saka, Lhasa and Batang in Tibet. The world's highest mountain, Mount Everest, lies slightly southward of the 30 degree meridian. Is it believed that Tibetan pyramids never attained the size of the "Cheops" Pyramid but they were distinguished by their multicolored sides, inscribed with tribal symbols with deep meaning to the people who constructed them.

As mentioned in later issues of the "The Pyramid Guide," the pyramid line advances eastward through China, not far south of the Shensi, Sian pyramids and Pan-P'O Village pyramid complex. Chung King and Shanghai are notably close to this circuitous, pyramid route. Continuing eastward across the Pacific Ocean, the world's ancient pyramid path advances below and lateral to the southern extremity of the Japanese mainland, north of, but very near to, the triangular-shaped "Devil's Sea." The line then slices eastward through a vast stretch of the open Pacific, intruding into and beyond the northern tip of the legendary sunken continent of "Mu." It was surely a land-base for two or more giant pyramids and countless smaller step pyramids, possibly predating all man-made pyramidal structures ever known. Midway Island, one of the last visible landmarks of the ancient continent of "Mu," lies slightly south of the 30° north parallel.

Notice how the pyramid belt projects a line across the meeting of land and sea along the northern shore of the Gulf of Lower California, as it also projects across a similar plane in the Persian Gulf, and continues this same characteristic in a line separating the U.S. mainland and the Gulf of Mexico, particularly at New Orleans. From there, the pyramid meridian cuts across St. Augustine, Florida. Then it progresses onward through the notorious Bermuda Triangle south of the Bermuda Islands, where Dr. Ray Brown discovered his seabed pyramid and crystal. This is also the general area of the greater pyramids recently found on the ocean floor off Florida. Moreover, it lies within a portion of the suspected lost continent of Atlantis and its sunken pyramids, indicating it is perhaps the site of the originating master pyramid, the initial model for the world's remaining pyramid structures found today.

From there, the belt literally runs across that vast, generally unoccupied expanse of the Atlantic Ocean to the Canary Islands; Ifni at Rio del Oro on the West Coast of Africa; Agadir, Morocco; thence to Beni Abbes, Algeria; to Gadames in Libya; onward across the southern tip of the Gulf of Sidra and back home to Cairo, Egypt, and the Great Pyramid, navel of the world.

A possible shift in the world's continents since ancient times may account for the Great Pyramid's present location at 29° 58' 51," less than one and one-half seconds variation from the actual 30 degree meridian.

Terry Allen of Los Angeles points out that the 30° parallels constitute the "Horse Latitudes." These dual lines surrounding our globe north and south of the equator form the edges of the trade wind belts. The Horse Latitudes are noted for their calming, light and variable winds and were apparently fatal to horses transported on ships from continent to continent.

Does a pyramid belt then encircle the earth at 30 degrees south latitude? Information verifying this possibility has not been forthcoming. It's easier to establish another possible pyramid belt in the vicinity of the equator, as evidenced by pyramids found in Africa, Ceylon, Cambodia, Polynesia and expected future findings in the southern tip of "Mu" in the Pacific.

Mexico, Central and South America, mostly north of the equator, have continuously revealed their large numbers of pyramids since the conquests of Cortez 450 years ago. Whether they fit into another larger encircling pattern remains to be seen, a mysterious possibility that, like so many other mysteries of the pyramids, continues to await its time.

Only the Sphinx knows.

Maria D'Andrea

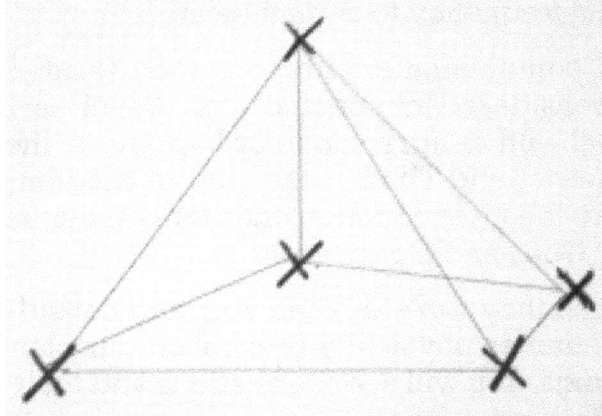

ALIENS AND THE PYRAMIDS

Rev. Maria D'Andrea, MsD, D.D., DRH

Through ancient times, we as European shamans have worked with the old ways, as other cultures have. We work with underground wisdom to help better people's lives and to help our people reach a Higher Understanding and to elevate everyone's life who is open to improving in a positive way.

Aliens have been among us and passing on knowledge through inter-dimensional communication since time unknown.

We were able (and still are) to communicate with them. At the time of Egypt, the pyramids were utilized for many purposes. One of them was to communicate with other beings not of this earth.

One such method was as follows:

Five magi would go into a deep meditation at a certain time and day depending on the placement of the constellations.

They would then place a headband made of a particular material over their heads and covering the third eye, with a terminated clear quartz crystal attached and pointing upward.

Four of the magi would stand at the corner of the base of the pyramid, four being the number for creating a foundation/base to build from spiritually and with physical alignment.

The fifth magi would stand as close to the top of the pyramid as possible, five being the number of changes and movement.

They would all, at the same time, raise their arms to the sky and, with mental/psychic focus, tune into the vibration of the alien energy to harness it and connect a link to communicate, much as tuning into a radio station by changing the dial until you get the right station frequency that you are looking for. In this manner they were able to send and receive messages. To this day, you will find magi/shamans and other spiritual adepts standing on mountains or higher elevations in order to be less disturbed by city and community interference and to be able to connect to that special frequency to communicate.

They would then communicate with what they termed deities or Spiritual Guides. Some were considered for specific intents, such as: Hathor – to gain information on how to deal with or attract love or happiness; the Goddess Maat – for cosmic order and justice; and Thoth – the God of wisdom. They all have other abilities, but these are the most common ones for communication reasons. Not to mention all the other Gods and Goddesses.

The magi knew who they were dealing with and considered the aliens inter-dimensional and sometimes physically present on our planet. If you look at ancient Egyptian drawings, you will see these aliens and their effect on society.

Many cultures have built pyramids. You will find them in locations very far from one another. At that time, people were not connected or were not in communication with each other as we are now, due to the great distances and the lack of the ability to travel the way we do.

The pyramids were also used as amplifiers. You can build a small pyramid now according to the specifications required. If you build it according to the exact measurements, you can use it to amplify and heighten energy.

The pyramids have a very high vibration. When you visit a pyramid site, it may not be something obvious, but some people feel a stronger connection to their soul. It may be a connection to their spirituality being awakened or heightened. It may be looked at as a trigger or amplifier so that, days or even weeks later, you may have an "aha" moment or just simply be more spiritual in your every day dealings.

The magi passed down their knowledge to initiates about the other worldly connections that we have. They taught how to open the doorway or portal to various dimensions and to other realms of reality.

Aliens can be positive or negative. You need to know how to energetically protect yourself with psychic self-defense before you venture out. After all, before you go on a car trip, don't you check that you have enough gas, air in your tires, and what the best time is to leave so you encounter better traffic, among other issues? Your soul needs to be safer. Hence, the defense.

The pictographs of the Gods and Goddesses in all cultures around the world have physical and spiritual common ground. They seem to have the pyramids as their base for many situations. They are said to vibrationally amplify the magi's powers, including communication with the other worldly beings.

The information from these alien beings was beneficial to the community and precipitated spiritual awakenings. As with all people with individual will, some people listened and some did not. Free will always overrides everything else, and this is as it is supposed to be.

The energy of the pyramids was said to speed up one's natural healing process. Even today, people build their pyramids with the correct materials and according to specific measurements, which vary depending on the pyramid's size. Some healers build one large enough to accommodate a person within the pyramid who can then heal more quickly and more completely than they would otherwise.

The Egyptians gained some of their great knowledge from the other worldly sources. They knew about the stars and aligned their pyramids toward the North Star. Exact numbers had to be known and utilized in all of the pyramids for the vibrational and energetic effects to work. How would so many different, non-connected cultures have the same knowledge? You must go "Hmmm"...

It is said that there are hidden underground rooms and passages under the pyramids and that there are communications sources and valued information we need in these catacombs. It is also said that the aliens who built these were extremely tall and large. David and Goliath reminders?

Another ancient magi wisdom was/is that:

The way to utilize these energies is to create a small pyramid (according to the right specifications) and sit or stand in the middle to reenergize/revitalize your body. Not as much for beauty (although it helps your skin to regenerate better), but for your overall physical health to be better and more vibrant.

On the physical side, there are very old drawings that showed giants among us. We have the story of the giant Goliath being killed by a stone that was thrown by a normal-sized youth named David. And how is it that the giants were drawn in those times by not just one culture? How is that possible? If it was simply a story of that time, in Egypt, how could other cultures tell the same type of tales without seeing the same source?

Other drawings depict what look like astronauts wearing spacesuits much like ours in order to breathe in space or on our planet. The drawings go back thousands of years. The pyramids are also said to "point the way," helping those looking down from space to locate possible landing sites. Now, why would they need landing sites at that time without planes or other flying machines? It makes you wonder. Some beings must have been in the skies at that time.

Pyramid power is very strong and unique. The more we learn, the more amazing it is, especially considering the pyramids were built thousands of years ago. The pyramids are still hiding great knowledge, and we are bound to find the wisdom through time and effort. We can already utilize some of the power. We need to see past the physical aspects and look for how to incorporate the soul/spiritual growth aspects so that we can apply them.

The spiritual elevation and wisdom concealed in the pyramids can bring new awareness and a better community of mankind to us. We simply need to work with the energies and learn how to incorporate these new (yet ancient) abilities in daily life.

Seek out this wisdom through books, energy work, travel, meditation or any modality that works for you. The Higher you are spiritually, the better your life is.

THE PYRAMIDS SPEAK

Tim Beckley and artist Carol Ann Rodriguez conceive of flying over a pyramid in Mexico onboard a mother ship piloted by ancient astronauts who have returned. (Inspirational art by Carol Ann Rodriguez).

PYRAMIDS FROM AROUND THE WORLD
WHY DOESN'T ARCHAEOLOGY ACKNOWLEDGE THEM?
By Timothy Green Beckley

I met Bruce under the "weirdest" of circumstances, which isn't that unusual for me considering the number of synchronicities and "coincidences" that intertwine in my life on a regular basis.

Now, we're talking 25 plus years ago, so don't expect the details to be one hundred percent accurate.

For a long while I had been out of touch with Bruce Raphael but found him recently residing in – of all places – China, where he is running a successful investment business.

When I first met Bruce he was working in the travel business. I had purchased a round trip ticket from this travel agency near Pennsylvania Station in New York, but somehow there was a mix-up. When I went to use the return portion of the ticket, for one reason or another I couldn't get on the plane and was now seeking a refund or credit . . . plus I was a bit mad about having been booted off a flight I should have been on.

The receptionist sent me to one of their agents, and so it was by "random selection" that I was given this nice young gentlemen, who didn't know me from Adam, to straighten the entire discombobulated matter out.

Amidst the idle chitchat while the agent was going over some paperwork to see what had gone wrong, the conversation turned to careers, and I revealed to the agent, who by this time had told me his name, that I ran a small publishing company that put out esoteric titles. I found that mentioning UFOs or the paranormal turned some people off or brought on too many questions, so I tried to keep it as general as possible. Bruce said something to the effect that that was interesting and I do believe we spoke about UFOs for maybe a whole thirty seconds or so.

Eventually, the ticket situation was corrected and I was on my way.

A couple of years later I was at the apartment of Marc and Phyllis Brinkerhoff

THE PYRAMIDS SPEAK

near Central Park. I think it was Marc's birthday. Marc is a fabulous artist who specializes in lifelike paintings of fairies, unicorns and golden-haired space beings of the Nordic type. Phyllis had been working for a local TV station when I introduced the two of them. They eventually got married, so I guess that makes me a matchmaker of sorts (among other things). As usual, Marc and Phyllis had gathered an eclectic group for the evening, one of whom I thought I recognized. Turns out it was the young man from the travel agency whom I had entirely forgotten about. With a glass of bubbly in our hands in a toast to Marc for his birthday, I asked Bruce what he was doing at a party for a fellow who had had multiple UFO sightings, had taken photos of unusual objects in the sky, and who claimed actual face to face meetings with aliens?

Bruce Raphael

Bruce muttered something about having picked up a book or two on the subject after our initial coincidental meeting at the travel agency. He had become fascinated with the subject and had drifted into the rather small New York City contingent of "extraterrestrials are amongst us" believers. This being years before I was sucked into believing that many of these synchronicities that we in the paranormal field experience have to be contended with regularly, we shared a bemused smile and separated company.

Not sure when, but the next time I ran into Bruce, things had even gotten a bit more bizarre. The former travel agent turned globetrotter had married a charming lady from Australia and they were out hob-nobbling the countryside Down Under in search of pyramids. Did I say pyramids?

Seems that Bruce and his lady Marilyn had been attending channeling sessions where the subject of pyramids came up.

But at this point let me turn the dialogue over to Bruce, who filed this report with me circa mid-1980s and which I published in the now defunct but still only "official" flying saucer newspaper, the **UFO Review.**

DO HOPI PROPHECIES HOLD KEY TO MYSTERIOUS ARTIFACT UNEARTHED AT SITE OF AUSTRALIAN PYRAMID?

A Research Report by Bruce Raphael

An unusual discovery of a strange artifact made halfway around the world has led an Australian woman to meet with representatives of an American Indian tribe in hopes of obtaining some answers linked to the origin and meaning of a mysterious 92 lb. rock showing a sun symbol and two serpents carved into one side.

On March 25, 1982, Marilyn Pye of Queensland was told while attending a psychic channeling session that a "golden pyramid" existed ninety miles north of Cairns, Australia. Within five weeks, Marilyn had sold her home, walked out of a newly-opened business and had retained the help of a well-known New York psychic, Bryce Bond, to help her unlock the secret of these pyramids which, at first, Australian archaeologists even refused to acknowledge the mere existence of. Responding to nationwide media coverage, Marilyn was led to the town of Toowoomba, Queensland, where a strange basalt crystal rock was unearthed beneath 24 feet of soil. Quite easily it was determined that this stone and its peculiar writing was not the work of aboriginal natives, though legends of the local tribes do tell of not one, but two "golden pyramids" in the near vicinity of this remarkable scientific find.

Packing the 92 lb. artifact in a special crate, Marilyn flew with her "precious cargo" first to Hawaii to meet with the Kahuna, who did a reading on the rock. They concluded that the engraving had been done 30,000 years ago with three different sized laser beams. They also said the rock was a "computer" which could be used to bring wisdom and peace to the world.

At this stage in her quest, Marilyn became aware of the Hopi prophecies concerning the return of the true "White Brother," which tells of a white person bringing the symbol of the sun to the Hopi. The Kahuna said there were three other rocks, while a Hopi representative told Marilyn that several engraved rocks exist on different continents and that they must come forth before the day of purification.

THE PYRAMIDS SPEAK

Marilyn sensed that she had to meet with the Hopi. Four days after arriving in New York, she was introduced to John Hill, an Iroquois Indian who was in Manhattan to speak at the United Nations regarding the "last days," which many Indians feel are approaching.

When Marilyn showed Mr. Hill the rock, he became very excited and arranged for many important people to view the artifact while Marilyn remained in the city. The effect on people was amazing. The rock seemed to be putting out incredibly beautiful energy. People would become light and very energized. Through a chain of events, the Hopi found out about the rock and were anxious to determine if, indeed, it was the missing rock from their prophecies.

Six days before Christmas, Marilyn decided to travel to Arizona, where she would meet with Medicine Men familiar with such religious and spiritual matters.

As can sometimes happen on cross-country jaunts, the journey turned into a nightmare. Planes were delayed. Flights were missed. Connections got crossed, but finally Marilyn and a Peruvian Indian traveling with her arrived at their destination (though only after the friend had been arrested for drunken driving because he had pulled over to the side of the road to rest up from the long drive). They both felt that some supernatural power was trying to prevent them from getting the rock to the Hopi.

It had been arranged for Marilyn to meet with Grandfather David, who is over 100 years old and blind. He felt the rock's engraving and became very excited. "This is what we have been waiting for. There are three others to come," is all he would say. Marilyn was asked to leave the rock behind so that the Hopi priests could take a closer look at it

The rock was returned to her six days later, after the Hopi had taken a rubbing of the artifact's surface to determine its origins and meaning. To date, the Hopi have remained tight-lipped about their findings, which has convinced Ms. Pye all the more that there is something to her startling discovery.

The story of the rock is apparently far from over. Marilyn dearly believes that there is much more to be said about this ROCK OF AGES and is now trying to get government support in her native Australia to dig for the golden pyramid(s), which she is convinced exist(s) in Australia and may have origins dating back thousands of years to a previous civilization that may have existed on this planet long before the time of Noah's flood. There is reason to believe the Hopi could help her unravel the pieces of this cosmic jigsaw puzzle.

* * * * *

As of this writing Ms Pye has vanished back into the underbrush. Her planned book on her discoveries of Australia's pyramids has never been forthcoming and her trilogy on Moses fell two volumes short. But, nevertheless, our quest has only begun as we travel the world in search of the mysteries of unknown pyramids. You are welcome to assist in our efforts to reveal their secrets.

RESEARCHER'S UPDATE

I received the following additional correspondence from Bruce Raphael as this book was being written:

"That study of how the grid lines around the Earth," Bruce says, "always had some value is part of the long history of cultures before and after Atlantis that used pyramids for storing Qi and moving Qi during certain cycles. I've included a picture of the Huang-Ti Mausoleum in the shape of a low sprawling pyramid mound that housed the King and his secrets. I have attached a work-sheet of notes on the new research and you'll notice that I began with the longitude of the Golden Meridian that coincides with the same longitude, 180 degrees, on the other side of the planet running through America into Banff Springs/Lake Louise, where a portal has been reported opening on a regular basis."

While public disclosure about the pyramid(s) in Australia has tapered off in the time since Ms. Pye has gone into seclusion, Bruce says he has continued on behind the scenes.

"Working silently from 1985 to the present, ensuring the evidence was verifiable and synchronized with current archaeological issues, I waited patiently for Marilyn to come to her conclusions and go public with her story. An important book to read is

Aerial view of the Huang-Ti Mausoleum

Oppenheimer's 'Eden of the East,' which outlines the basic theory that the Earth's cataclysms from around 8000 BCE contributed to a science of the 'dreaming,' a world myth that required a rebuilding of the balance between heaven and earth, earth weather metastability, seasonal variation and cultural resettlement as depicted by the search for new territories by cultures in collision as represented by the myths of the twins, brothers or variant bloodlines as in the Cain and Abel story.

THE PYRAMIDS SPEAK

"Oppenheimer was aware of very little news of our lost civilization issues here in Australia, with much of his extensive research pointing to New Guinea and the Polynesian express theory, Lapita culture evidence, and the spread of a metaphysical heritage from Southeast Asia into the West. Australian ethnographers are well aware of the role of the Rainbow Serpent in Aboriginal legends about the flood epic. Many legends record the disappearance of the moon and sky.

"The action of great flooding brought about the collapse of the Sundra Shelf and hence sent further maritime expeditions away from the coastlines of Vietnam, China and Thailand. The question of South American and Middle Eastern presence is an additional string in a long chain of events that brought many entradas to Australia.

"Keeping in touch with Marilyn Pye and her story has been an ongoing pursuit since 1984 when I first came to Australia to look at the evidence. I tracked her activities in my journal for over 15 years, trying to keep an accurate record of her movements and acquisitions. Her relaunch of her theory and findings will contribute greatly now to a new millennium of controversy.

"Her quest to find and discover the Golden Pyramid along with her quiet digs and geological surveys in Cooktown is where the story truly begins. I spent the last 10 years mapping and surveying sites that were connected in energy-grid dynamics to the Cooktown question and found some amazing results. Cathian Lunar Grid, to mention the most popular.

"Since 1984, I had many correspondences with Bruce Cathie and in one of them he assisted me in getting started on how the data stacked up in grid math. The sites are: Ayers Rock (Marker R), Aboriginal Stonehenge (Marker H), Marilyn's site (Marker B), and Marker E-Series the Astronomical Observatory at Mt. Carbine.

"In my book, 'Rhythms in the Landscape,' I inform the reader that if an ancient race were able to position any of these sites correctly on existing grid lines, they would do so by using a language that was not quite music, not quite alphabet, as we know it. An American epigrapher and rock-art researcher Charles Boyle had put forth a new process in the chapter of 'reading the record accurately' of ancient stone writings and megalithic statements. His focus was on the Gaelic science of Teanga. This, he stated, could be worked into any language, so it was universal — a solar-based wisdom. So I was able to view the math evidence with linguistic patterns using Cathie and Boyle as a mainframe."

EVEN MORE PYRAMIDS
FROM AROUND THE WORLD

By Sean Casteel

AUSTRALIA'S GYMPIE PYRAMID

The Gympie Pyramid is a low-terraced structure located in the outskirts of Gympie in Queensland. A man named Rex Gilroy claims that he discovered the Gympie Pyramid in 1975, declaring that the pyramid was created by Egyptians who had mining operations in Australia centuries ago, with bases of operations reaching as far as the Blue Mountains in New South Wales.

But author Brett J. Green offers a slightly different account. According to Green, the first recorded pioneer evidences of an old "ruins complex" in the area appeared sometime between 1860 and 1880. Such "evidences" were later verified when there was a desperate need for sandstone blocks for commercial building following the Gympie Gold Rush days of 1867. Local business operators and opportunists learned that there was a place in the jungle with vast quantities of pre-shaped sandstone blocks ready for "recycling." Thus the building blocks of the pyramidal structure, what the locals called "piles of rocks," were pilfered for houses, fireplaces and commercial establishments. By 1885, the entire site was devoid of any past existence.

To any current viewer, the vestiges of past antiquity cannot be seen. All that remains is a stone-covered, lightly forested hill soon to be erased by encroaching housing developments. Green calls it a "legacy of pure stupidity" and bemoans the fact that what may have been Australia's most valuable ancient site and the only clue to a very ancient past has been so irresponsibly destroyed.

But Marilyn Pye, also mentioned in Bruce Raphael's article above, became convinced that the pyramid was evidence of ancient settlement in Australia by the Incas of South America. There are believed to have been local legends and taboos that warned against intrusion into the pyramid area. Found nearby was a

THE PYRAMIDS SPEAK

statue depicting an "Iron Man" or "Gympie Ape" said to be of non-aboriginal manufacture that perhaps bolster Pye's argument. Other strange statues were found in the area and removed for examination by "authorities" in Queensland and never returned, though photographs of the statues still exist.

Meanwhile, British author Gavin Menzies states that the Gympie Pyramid is "direct and persuasive evidence of the Chinese visits to Australia" and that its size, height and shape are typical of Ming Dynasty observation platforms. "It would have been wholly logical for the Chinese to build observatories to determine precisely the location of the phenomenal riches they had discovered," Menzies writes, presumably referring to the large quantities of gold the region once contained.

Debunkers of a less mystical bent have speculated the Gympie Pyramid may have been built by an Italian farmer to stop erosion on a natural mesa on his property. Another theory proposes that the terraced structure was erected by a Swiss horticulturist in the late 1880s. In spite of decades of vigorous controversy, especially in the Australian media, the Gympie Pyramid remains a mystery.

PYRAMIDS IN MEXICO AND CENTRAL AMERICA

"Just north of Mexico City," says a travel website called Viator.com, "are the mysterious Teotihuacan Pyramids, built beginning around 300 B.C. as the centerpiece of an enormous city, often compared to ancient Rome. They were inexplicably abandoned centuries before the arrival of the Aztecs, who called the ancient architectural marvel the 'Birthplace of the Gods.'"

The landscape of the ancient city of Teotihuacan is dominated by the Pyramid of the Sun, which is the third largest pyramid in the world and stands over 230 feet high. Nearby is a long and broad avenue called the "Street of the Dead," a main thoroughfare that led to other pyramids and temples and was lined with fine civic and religious buildings.

Teotihuacan was a highly organized city rigidly governed by religious and secular leaders who maintained an iron grip on the minds, spirits and bodies of their subjects. The priests were its intellectual elites and were also skillful astronomers who kept track of the procession of days, months and years by observing the stars.

The Pyramid of the Moon is the second largest pyramid in Teotihuacan and is located in the western part of the city. It is said to "mimic" the contours of the nearby Cerro Gordo Mountain. Its name is sometimes translated as "mother or protective stone." The Pyramid of the Moon was constructed sometime between 200 and 450 A.D. and also has easy access to the Street of the Dead. The structure was dedicated to the Great Goddess, who they believed to be the source of water, fertility, the Earth and creation itself. In the late 1990s, separate teams of archeologists discovered within the pyramid the skeletons of human and animal sacrificial victims as well as jewelry, obsidian blades and over 400 other relics.

No one knows the exact ethnicity of the people who built Teotihuacan nor what happened to end their civilization. Some historians believe the city was struck by some great catastrophe around 700 A.D. that greatly reduced its population and caused many to migrate eastward. There is evidence that the city was deliberately burnt and destroyed, after which some of its buildings collapsed and the pyramids became overgrown with dense vegetation. Teotihuacan is nevertheless still revered as an intensely sacred place, though its builders and residents have long ago disappeared into the mists of history.

The Mayans, by contrast, are a people whose ethnicity and history are a little easier to fathom. The pyramids built by the Mayans stand out as one of the most impressive architectural achievements of the ancient world, being designed with great precision and requiring a massive human effort to build. They offer testimony that the Mayans were a highly organized society capable of unique accomplishments in language, astronomy and mathematics but one that also carried out human sacrifice and gruesome blood rituals. Their civilization stretched from the Yucatan Peninsula in southern Mexico to present-day Honduras and El Salvador.

Australian Pyramid

THE PYRAMIDS SPEAK

A typical Mayan pyramid was a series of stepped platforms with a small temple built on top. Steep stairways lined the sides of the pyramids to allow the priests to climb to the top to conduct various rituals. When it was deemed necessary to keep a given ritual secret, it would be conducted in a room located inside the pyramid.

The pyramids could reach as high as 230 feet above the ground. As in Egypt, some pyramids served as burial chambers for kings. Others were designed precisely to mark the equinox and solstice positions of the sun at sunrise. But the majority of the Mayan pyramids were dedicated to honor and appease the gods through human sacrifice and bloodletting.

PYRAMIDS IN CHINA

The pyramids in China are open to some dispute. Nowadays, no one really doubts their existence, but there have been instances where the Chinese government has simply refused to acknowledge the unique structures are even there.

Early stories about the pyramids in China began right around the Second World War. A U.S. Air Force pilot reportedly saw a white-topped pyramid during a flight between China and India in 1945. He described the pyramid as looking "like something out of a fairy tale," being "encased in shimmering white on all sides." The pyramid had a remarkable jewellike capstone that could have been crystal. He recalls that he and the whole flight crew were awed by the pyramid's sheer size. The pilot photographed the White Pyramid with the same camera he'd just used to photograph troop movements, but later groups of searchers have never been able to rediscover its location.

The world's largest pyramid is rumored to be in Qin Lin county in a "forbidden zone" of China. It is estimated to be 1,000 feet high, making it twice as large as the Great Pyramid at Giza. Some experts believe the Chinese pyramids – and there could be more than 100 of them – share mathematical characteristics with the pyramids in Egypt and may even have been built by the same people.

PYRAMIDS IN THE UNITED STATES

Around 200 A.D., indigenous peoples in Florida and Georgia began the construction of enormous earthen pyramids. One such earthen pyramid was built in the Florida panhandle at a site known today as the Letchworth-Love Mounds. The pyramid is the tallest such earthwork in Florida at over 46 feet high.

Across the border in Georgia is another huge earthen pyramid erected at the same time as the Letchworth-Love edifice. The Georgia site is called the Kolomoki Mounds, and the largest pyramid there has a base larger than a football field and rises 57 feet high.

There is disagreement among mainstream archeologists regarding exactly who actually built these American pyramids, but they point to a long tradition of mound building in the southeast and these sites may be simply a natural evolution of various preexisting cultures. While it is true that Florida's Indians, for example, had constructed small sand and shell burial mounds for thousands of years, those in no way compare to the scale and complexity of Letchworth-Love.

Poverty Point is located fifteen miles from the Mississippi River near the village of Epps in West Carroll Parish in northeastern Louisiana. Comprised of several earthworks and mounds built between 1650 and 700 B.C., they are credited to a group of Native-Americans simply called the "Poverty Point Culture" since further details of their identity remain unknown to present-day archeologists. The earthworks are spread out over 910 acres and have been described as "the largest and most complex Late Archaic earthwork occupational and ceremonial site yet found in North America." Poverty Point was brought to the attention of archeologists in the early 20th century and named after a nearby plantation. Scholars have advanced various theories as to its purpose, with some concluding it was most likely used for religious or ceremonial rites.

John A. Ward, in his 1984 book, "Ancient Archives Among The Cornstalks," claimed that Poverty Point was built by refugees fleeing up the Mississippi River after their home, Atlantis, was destroyed in 1198 B.C. Erich von Daniken has suggested that one of the mounds there was a landing platform for alien aircraft.

JAPAN'S ANCIENT UNDERWATER PYRAMID

The Yonaguni Pyramid is a massive underwater rock formation off the coast of Yonaguni, the southernmost of the Ryukyu Islands, in Japan. There is debate about whether the site is completely natural, is a natural site that has been modified, or is a man-made artifact. It was discovered by accident in 1987 by a Japanese tourism director who was looking for a good place to observe sharks in the area. He noticed some singular seabed formations resembling architectonic structures. Soon after, a team of scientists from the University of Ryukyus visited the area.

The main feature is a rectangular formation measuring about 490 feet by 130 feet, and about 90 feet tall. The top is about 16 feet below sea level. The flat parallel faces, sharp edges and mostly right angles of the pyramid have led many people, including many of the underwater photographers, divers and scholars who have visited the site, to conclude that those features are man-made.

Masaaki Kimura, the leader of the university team, spent more than 15 years studying the Yonaguni Pyramid and told the National Geographic in 2007 that he believed the site was actually part of the ruins of Mu, a fabled Pacific civilization said to have vanished beneath the waves thousands of years ago in a manner similar to Atlantis. Kimura said the main structure "looks like a complicated, monolithic, stepped pyramid that rises from a depth of 82 feet."

While many argue that Yonaguni Pyramid is a purely natural structure, Kimura counters that he has identified quarry marks in its stones, as well as rudimentary characters etched onto carved faces and rocks sculpted into the likenesses of animals. There are other underwater structures in the area, to include the ruins of a castle, a triumphal arch, five temples and a large stadium, all of which are connected by roads and water channels.

* * * * * *

While the pyramids of Egypt hold a fascination for archeologists and historians that will likely endure as long as the mysterious edifices themselves, one should also be aware that there are other pyramid structures found throughout the world. The fact that the same sort of precisely mathematically-aligned structures were built by ancient societies who could not possibly have been in contact with one another leads many to theorize that the pyramids were not simply man-made but were erected with a little alien help.

THE PYRAMIDS SPEAK

The foundation of this massive ziggurat—The Tower of Babel—
can be seen in Southern Iraq

Boraippa, Iraq - December 3, 1998 - Associated Press

After 20 years of digging, Austrian archaeologists say they have determined the design of a Mesopotamian ziggurat - a temple tower - built by King Nebuchadnezzar some 2,500 years ago. The temple tower consisted of seven terraces built of millions of mud bricks and rose 231 feet, the scientists say. It probably was similar to the many ziggurats built by Nebuchadnezzar, the ruler who ordered the destruction of the ancient Jewish temple in Jerusalem, they add.

The temple of Borsippa, 75 miles south of Baghdad, was constructed atop the ruins of a smaller tower from the second millennium B.C. Nebuchadnezzar's temple was dedicated to Nabu, the god of science and learning in Mesopotamia and the king's protector. Wilfrid Allinger-Csollich of the University of Innsbruck said that of all the temple towers built during the Nebuchadnezzar's 40-year reign, the Borsippa ziggurat has best survived the ravages of time.

The Austrians removed thousands of tons of debris from the mound that gradually built up around the tower over the ages and uncovered most of the ziggurat's remains, which still rise to 172 feet. The work revealed the tower's exact dimensions, Allinger-Csollich said. "We did not use high-tech, but rudimentary means. We just counted the number of bricks," he said.

The square bricks used by Nebuchadnezzar had standard dimensions — 13 1/4 inches on each side and 3 1/4 inches in depth. The Austrians used mechanical shovels to reach the foundation, which they measured at 297 by 297 feet.

More than 1 million fired bricks were used for the first level's 3.3-foot-tall outer wall, Allinger-Csollich said. Given the Borsippa tower's height of 231 feet. The builders filled the inside of each level with tens of millions of unfired bricks held in place with cedar beams brought from Lebanon.

The Austrians determined the tower had three staircases and are in the process of calculating how many steps each had. Their picture of the temple's exterior is almost complete. The first two levels were covered with bitumen and were black. The third, fourth and fifth were decorated with blue-glazed bricks and possibly adorned with bulls and lions. The sixth and seventh terraces, close to the sanctuary, were wholly made of mud brick. For cultic purposes the Mesopotamians thought mud to be the purest of substances. On top was Nabu's residence with rooms for servants and priests and wings for his wife, Tachmitum, his children and daughters.

There must have been a big library of cuneiform tablets. Among the finds are several tablets and a foundation stone with inscriptions detailing why and how Nebuchadnezzar constructed the tower in Borsippa. One text says the king wanted the Borsippa built on the same design as that of the Tower of Babel, of which only the foundation survives in Babylon seven miles to the north. Another text quotes Nebuchadnezzar as declaring that Nabu's tower should reach the skies and be no less in grandeur than that of Babel, which was dedicated to the god Marduk.

Famous Ziggurat: The Tower of Babel in Southern Iraq

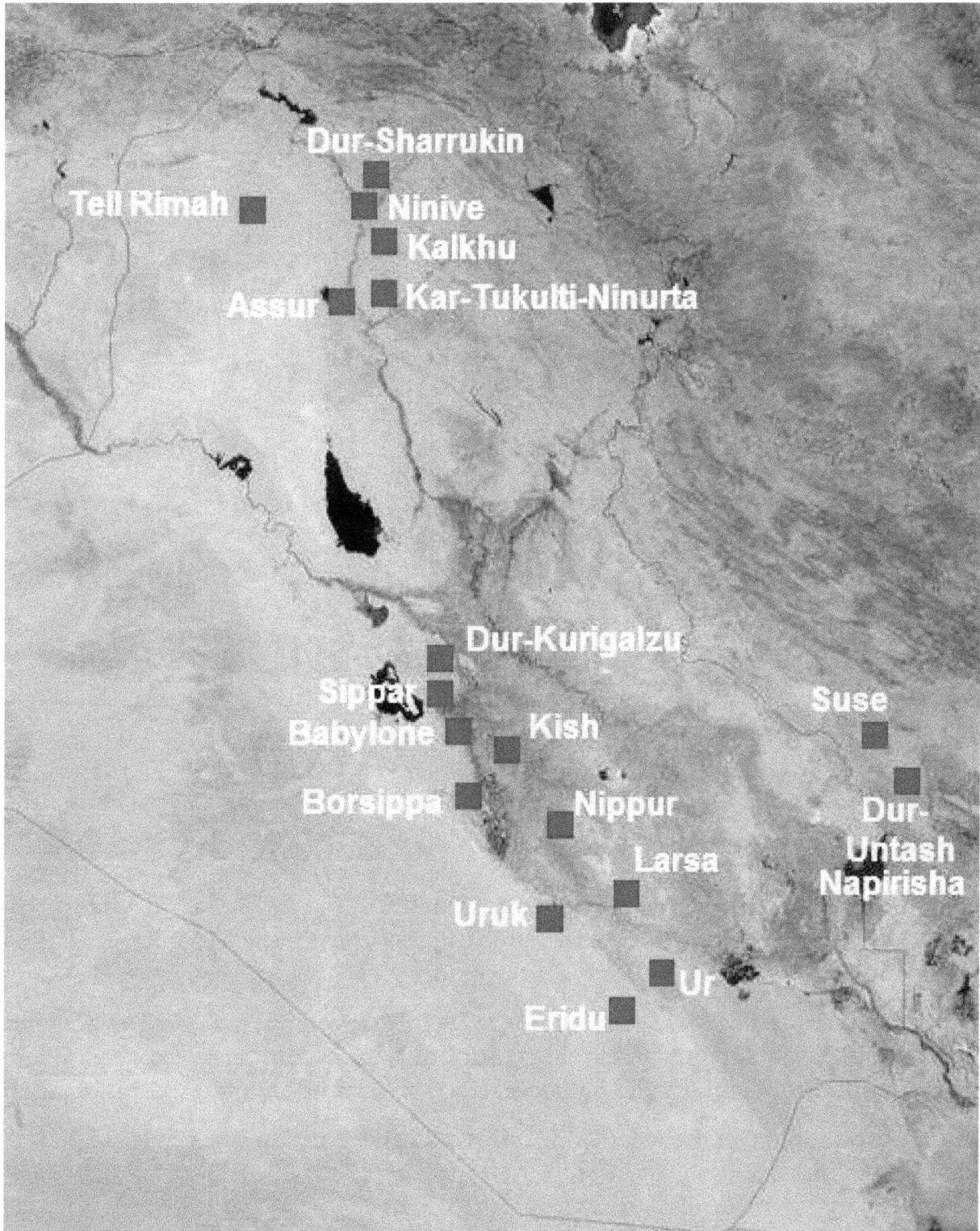

Known locations of ziggurats in Iraq

THE PYRAMIDS SPEAK

Pyramid Mounds In North America

The Adena Culture thrived from circa 1000 BC to 200 AD, and were centered in the Ohio Valley. They were localized into current-day Kentucky, Ohio, West Virginia, Indiana, Pennsylvania, and southwestern New York.

They cultivated several crops: gourds, including pumpkins, sunflowers, and goosefoot. They also cultivated tobacco, probably for ceremonial purposes. While these people were hunters and gatherers, they were predominantly non-nomadic.

The abundance of these lands permitted a sedentary existence.

THE PYRAMIDS SPEAK

PYRAMID KIT

The ancients were familiar with the power of the pyramid shape and how it could be used as an energy accumulator and to preserve. In recent years parapsychologists worldwide have tested the pyramid and found to their amazement that even miniature pyramids made to scale can produce some pretty astounding results when used under proper conditions.

The pyramid form on the inside back cover is of the proper dimensions to conduct such experiments on your own. It is not necessary to cut this book to use the pyramid. Simply trace the form exactly onto the sheet of ordinary paper and then paste it onto cardboard such as the type that comes with most men's dress shirts, or onto cover stock. Once you have done so you can begin to conduct your own experiments in the area of pyramid energy Below are just a few of the experiments you can conduct in your spare time.

1. Researchers have shown that food tends to taste better when kept under a pyramid. Try some cheese, fresh vegetables, fruit, or anything else you normally enjoy and see if there is a difference.

2. Tests have shown that it's easy to reconstitute stale orange juice.

3 You can keep your razor blades sharp almost forever if you keep them under a.pyramid. Try it with a new blade and see how long it will last compared to normal.

4. Pyramids have a positive effect on the temperature, making it possible to grow tomatoes and oranges even in the dead of winter while under pyramids. Even if you don't have a large enough pyramid to try such an experiment, try it out on a favorite flower in your yard and see if it doesn't last longer into the fall or even winter.

5. Investigators claim that if you put an old coin under a pyramid and leave it there for a month it will be restored to its original condition and a pile of rust will form nearby.

6. At least one individual who lives on the side of a mountain in California was having trouble with his TV reception, but when he used a metal pyramid as a TV antenna his reception improved one hundred percent.

7. For nine years the author of this book, Bill Cox, has been driving a car with a small pyramid mounted on the dash board and not only does he get extra miles to the gallon, but has never had any problems with the motor, nor does he have to change oil often.

8. Want to improve the taste of an inexpensive wine? Keep it under the pyramid for a few days and notice if there is a difference.

9. The yolk of an egg is said to take much longer to spoil if the egg is kept under a pyramid instead of being placed in the refrigerator.

10. Many researchers are convinced that the dunces cap or witches hat is based on the design of the pyramid, and that if you wear your pyramid on your head it may improve psychic ability or even cause you to feel more healthy. The next time you have a headache see if it doesn't take the pain away.

It has been noted, that in order for these experiences to work it is necessary to have a positive attitude towards these matters. Skeptics have poorer results than those who conduct such tests with an open mind.

Good luck in your own experimentation.

THE PYRAMIDS SPEAK

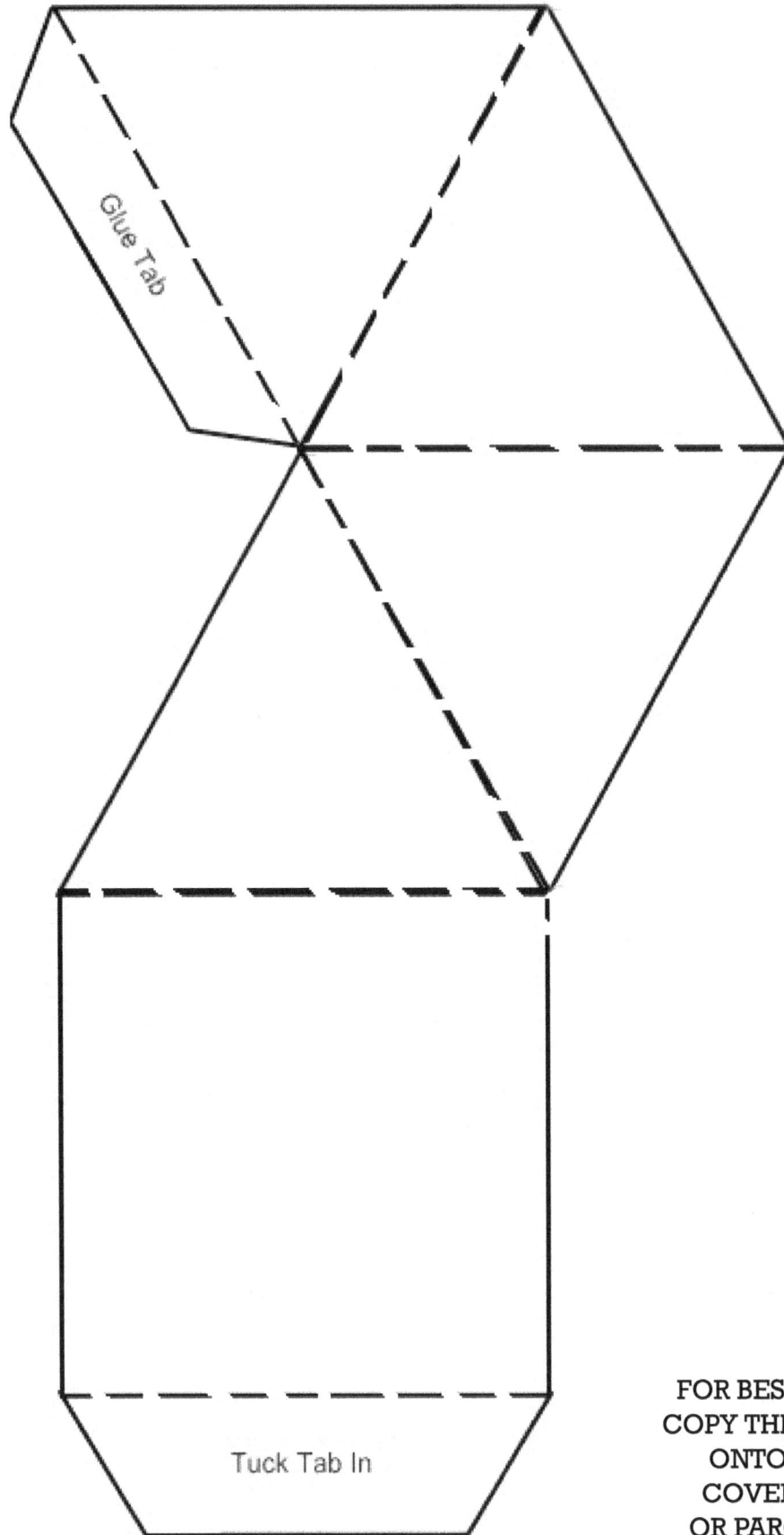

Glue Tab

Tuck Tab In

FOR BEST RESULTS
COPY THIS PYRAMID
ONTO HEAVY
COVER STOCK
OR PARCHMENT.

160